By

Edson B. "Ed" Waite, Jr.

A collection of incredible deer and the story of
the hunt, taken from interviews with the hunters
themselves, as published in various Buckmasters
publications.

This book is dedicated to:

Justin "Cole" Foglesong

13 May 1985 ~ 8 April 2006

Aged: 20 Yrs 10 Mo & 27 Days

Cover photo is the Cole Foglesong buck

Foreword

Ed Waite was plugged into Ohio's antler circuit long before social media and smart phones made life easier for deer detectives. While most measurers simply wait for hunters to call or come to them, Ed has never been content to settle for a ring or a knock. If he hears about an outstanding buck in his region, he's going to do his best to put a tape to it. And if he can't, he'll steer people toward nearer scorers.

In addition, if a hunter wants to share his or her story, Ed will likely stay yet another hour to hear it. Nobody has put more deer into our record book, and no other writer has produced as many stories about the Buckeye State's cream of the crop.

Ed's dedication to scoring and chronicling the tales behind Ohio's best whitetails are why he is a master scorer and regional director for Buckmasters Whitetail Trophy Records – positions for which he draws no salary. He, like all volunteer BTR measurers (many of whom he's trained), is in the game for the love of antlers.

Unlike most authors in this industry, Ed does not claim to be a deer hunting expert. He doesn't tell people how to hunt, doesn't endorse products, and he frowns if someone refers to him as legendary. Instead, he enables readers to learn from those who have experienced the highs and lows of chasing world-class whitetails, the ones who connect either because of hard work or through sheer luck.

I'm thrilled my friend has decided to share this definitive collection of stories. It will be one of the few deer hunting books I'll cherish.

Mike Handley, editor

Rack magazine

My scoring career began in the spring of 1995 when I became a Certified Scorer for Buckmasters Whitetail Trophy Records. (BTR)

During these 19 plus years I have measured in excess of 3,000 sets of antlers and sheds

As of the publication date of this book, I have measured more than 1,000 racks that meet the minimum score for entry in Buckmasters Whitetail Trophy Records.

Five of those deer carried racks exceeding 300 inches of antler, all were free roaming deer. (None will be featured in this book as I was not the author of the stories that appeared in the Buckmasters publications.)

For reference, below are the minimum requirements for entry into the Buckmasters Whitetail Trophy Records.

All numbers DO NOT include the inside spread!

All Archery ~ ~ ~ ~ 105 inches
All Firearms ~ ~ ~ ~ 140 inches
Shed antlers ~ ~ ~ ~ 75 inches per side
All Pickups ~ ~ ~ ~ 140 Inches (deer not harvested)

The Comp or Composite score shown on the score sheets includes the inside spread.

Buckmasters Full Credit scoring system does not take deductions, nor do they require any drying period.

Table of Contents

Freshman Gets an "A" in Hunting

Cole Foglesong Buck *

Photo courtesy Ed Waite

Nineteen-year-old Cole Foglesong of Astoria, Ill., a freshman biology student at McMurry College, has already made an impressive mark in the deer hunting world – thanks to an incredible 13-point buck he took during the Land of Lincoln's 2003 season.

While hunting on his family's property in Fulton County in 2001, Cole found an incredibly large shed from a buck known to inhabit the area. Some time and distance later, a neighbor found the other side of this once massive rack. No one knew the whereabouts of the buck that had worn it. It was never seen during the 2002 season.

"There is a lot of hunting pressure in this area, all during the season. I had even heard that the buck had been killed, but nobody could or would say how or by whom. It might have been hit by a car, when the antlers were off ... Who knows? It just vanished," Cole said.

The buck was not seen again until Nov. 22, 2003, the first day of shotgun season.

It was a beautiful autumn day, though warm. The temperature eventually climbed almost to 70 degrees. Cole was a bit late getting to the woods due to some pressing issues on the family farm. He was finally situated just after daylight in a concealed ground hideaway in the large swamp on the family-owned Black Gold Ranch in western Illinois.

"I have been hunting this area for several years. It is one of my favorite places to hunt. I had a treestand nearby for bowhunting, but I like to stay on the ground for shotgun season, and there was plenty of good cover nearby," Cole explained.

He had been watching and listening for quite some time, but had seen nothing. Around 9:30, he heard a noise off to the side and came to full alert.

"I spotted a very large deer moving from the swamp toward a nearby pasture field. There had been quite a few gunshots in the surrounding area, and the deer were feeling the pressure," he said. "At first, I wasn't sure if it was a buck or not, but it was a very large deer, so I prepared for the shot if it came close enough. When it passed through an open area, I saw enough to know it was a buck – a big one!"

The deer continued angling toward the hunter and finally stepped into the clear at a mere 15 yards. Cole raised the 12 gauge and prepared to send a rifled slug on its way. The deer was coming in broadside, a perfect target.

"When the buck was in the open, I forced myself not to look at the antlers. I aimed at the vitals, slipped off the safety and squeezed the trigger," Cole said. "I must have been too close or shaking some because I hit the deer higher than I planned. The slug cut the spine, and it dropped right there.

"I walked right over to the downed buck as it was still moving but not going anywhere. I watched as the life went out of it. I stared at the rack. It was huge, just HUGE – bigger than I could have imagined. I sat and stared at the antlers and the beautiful drop tine that was more than 11 inches long. I counted the points twice.

"Right away, I knew that it was the same buck whose sheds we'd found two years earlier. The antlers looked exactly the same, just a whole lot bigger!

"After a good 15 minutes, I decided it was time to tell the family, so I got out the two-way and radioed that I had a nice buck down. I didn't want them to know it was a monster, so I played it down as I told them exactly where I was and asked Dad to be sure to bring the camera.

"I guess Dad knew from the sound of my voice that it was more than just a small deer, but he and my brothers were all surprised at the size when they finally joined me. Lots of handshakes and high-fives were swapped, and lots of 'Hootin' and hollerin' followed before Dad took some pictures," declared Cole. "I don't think there were any deer left for miles around from all the hollering that I was doing. I was really excited!

"Lots of people showed up at the check station to get a close look at my deer. Field-dressed, it weighed 205 pounds, and this was AFTER the peak of the rut," Cole continued. "It was still in pretty good shape, physically, and none of the points were broken."

*Cole died of melanoma cancer less than two years after this story was written

Photo courtesy Ed Waite

Justin "Cole" Foglesong Buck

13

Official Buckmasters Score Sheet		
Taken by:	Cole Foglesong	
Date:	November 22, 2003	
Location:	Fulton Co., Illinois	
Method:	Shotgun	
Classification:	Semi-Irregular	
Measurements:	**Right**	**Left**
Total Points Side	6	7
Irregular Points Side	1	2
Total Irregular Inches	1 1/8	11 2/8
Length of Main Beam	26 6/8	25 4/8
Length of 1st Point	5 4/8	5 1/8
Length of 2nd Point	14 4/8	14 3/8
Length of 3rd Point	13 1/8	13 5/8
Length of 4th Point	7 5/8	9 3/8
Length of 5th Point		
Length of 6th Point		
1st Circumference (C1)	6	6
2nd Circumference (C2)	4 7/8	4 6/8
3rd Circumference (C3)	5 4/8	5 4/8
4th Circumference (C4)	5	5 5/8
Score Per Side	90	101 1/8
OFFICIAL SCORE	191 1/8	
Inside Spread	21 6/8	
COMPOSITE SCORE	212 7/8	
Percentage of Irregularity	6.5%	

Mirage and Mayhem
Lorain County root-wad buck is number 15 in a class filled with 200-inchers
Kevin Fitch Buck

Photo courtesy Kevin Fitch

It was as if the ground opened up and swallowed Kevin Fitch's buck. One minute, it was on the receiving end of a shotgun slug (he hoped). The next, it was gone. Not fall-down-dead gone.

Not running-with-the-wind-and-leaving-a-blood-trail gone.

Just gone, leaving the hunter from Norwalk, Ohio, with Rodney Dangerfield eyes and a mouth full of bile.

Seconds earlier, Kevin had finally seen antlers atop one of the 20 or so deer zigzagging in the brush ahead of him. He didn't have much of a window, but he thought the shot was doable.

"I was scanning heads, and, suddenly, I saw antlers. When they passed through an opening, followed by the head and neck of their wearer -- other than that, all I could see was the top of its back -- I slipped off the safety and squeezed the trigger," he said. "After the shot, the buck simply vanished. It didn't run off, and I didn't actually see it fall.

"It just disappeared," he added.

That was the first decent buck Kevin had seen in 2010, and now he wasn't seeing it.

"The archery season had been a bust for me," he said. "I never saw a buck I wanted to shoot. Actually, I was more interested in helping my 12-year-old son, Kyle, get a deer. We accomplished that task when he shot a very nice 130-inch buck from my favorite bow setup during the youth gun hunt."

Mission accomplished, Kevin was able to return his attention to his own tag, although work kept interfering. He pinned his hopes on the first day of Ohio's gun season, when he and some friends were going to Egypt Valley.

"But I never saw a deer the whole day," he said, "and I didn't get any more time in the woods the rest of the gun season."

Two weeks later, Ohio offered a bonus weekend for hunters who still had unfilled tags. Kevin, his son, Cody, and friend Dave and his dad qualified.

They had permission to hunt a 35-acre farm in Lorain County, not far from Kevin's home. The farm was virtually surrounded by CRP land, so it was like a haven for deer.

Kevin and Cody shared one ground blind, while Dave and his dad went to another. They'd set up the blinds the previous day, and were huddled inside on Saturday, Dec. 18, thankful for the thin barrier against the 13-degree cold.

"There was about three inches of snow on the ground, so getting in was a bit crunchy," Kevin said. "Cody and I hunkered down for the morning, but it wasn't long after daylight when my legs told me it was time to get up and start walking. I'm pretty tall and being crouched down in the crowded blind was hurting big time!

"The blind was set up on a low ridge overlooking a river bottom surrounded by thicket. Because the wind was driving straight north, I decided to loop around through the brush to see if I could jump some deer," he continued.

"Not long after I'd turned to get the wind in my face, I saw several does moving back and forth about 70 to 80 yards in front of me. I continued still-hunting through the briars and grapevines, and then I saw more lots more deer!

"I think the few had run right into the bedding area and disturbed everyone," Kevin added.

"I was scanning heads in every direction, looking for bucks, when I saw a glint of antler. It was in heavy cover, but I was sure it was antler so I keyed on that one deer.

"I tried not to lose sight of it as it moved among the trees and the other deer. Eventually, the buck began moving away from me, and I started looking for a shooting lane," he said.

Kevin found one opening and used a nearby cherry tree for a rest. When the deer stepped into it, he shot.

And that's when it disappeared.

While Kevin crept forward, he heard Cody shoot. Had he not heard strange whooshing sounds in front of him, he might've thought his son had shot at the same buck.

"The noise was coming from behind a blowdown with a large root system exposed," he said. "When I rounded the roots, I saw the spine-hit buck. It had fallen into and was trying to get out of the hole left by the roots. The hole was easily 10 feet across and half filled with frozen water.

"I had to do something. All I could think about was the deer breaking those huge antlers," he continued. "Finally, I got an angle and shot up through the vitals. Unfortunately, although it was a good shot, it only slowed the deer.

"My mind racing, I just grabbed the deer's head and pinned it to the ground. Ten minutes later, I let go and climbed out of the hole.

"Since I couldn't drag it out of there, I decided

to count points. I came up with like 30, at first. It was the biggest rack I had ever seen in the woods," he said.

Kevin was thoroughly juiced. He ran around in circles. And by the time he realized he should go for the four-wheeler in his truck, he had no idea in which direction to walk.

"I had gotten myself so excited and turned around, I didn't know which way to go," he said. "I didn't want to leave the deer, but I couldn't move it. Nor could I even tell anyone where I was at that point."

Kevin took off his gloves and cap and hung them on the antlers before seeking higher ground. About the time he saw his truck, Dave called to see what all the fuss was about.

"He knew I was only going to shoot a buck, so he figured I had shot and missed because he'd heard three shots," Kevin said. "He also told me that the biggest deer in the woods had just fled the scene, so there wasn't much use in continuing the hunt.

"I told him the biggest deer had not left the woods," he added.

Dave had indeed seen a very large buck. It had run out with some does, and his gun misfired. He watched the whole bunch cross a mile of CRP.

Kevin met Dave at the truck. They unloaded the ATV and drove in to pull his buck out of the hole.

"As we struggled to get the buck on the trailer, the landowner's daughter-in-law came out and took several pictures. She sent them to a few friends, many of whom came to look at it," he said.

Photo courtesy Kevin Fitch

Kevin Fitch Buck

Official Buckmasters Score Sheet		
Taken by:	**Kevin Fitch**	
Date:	**December 18, 2010**	
Location:	**Lorain Co., Ohio**	
Method:	**Shotgun**	
Classification:	**Irregular**	
Measurements:	**Right**	**Left**
Total Points Side	**12**	**11**
Irregular Points Side	**7**	**5**
Total Irregular Inches	**13 1/8**	**22 3/8**
Length of Main Beam	**27 1/8**	**26 4/8**
Length of 1st Point	**8 1/8**	**10 5/8**
Length of 2nd Point	**11 4/8**	**12 5/8**
Length of 3rd Point	**11 1/8**	**12**
Length of 4th Point	**8 2/8**	**7 4/8**
Length of 5th Point		**2 3/8**
Length of 6th Point		
1st Circumference (C1)	**6 6/8**	**5 6/8**
2nd Circumference (C2)	**5 4/8**	**5 6/8**
3rd Circumference (C3)	**5 3/8**	**5 4/8**
4th Circumference (C4)	**4 2/8**	**5 4/8**
Score Per Side	**101 1/8**	**116 4/8**
OFFICIAL SCORE	**217 5/8**	
Inside Spread	**21 2/8**	
COMPOSITE SCORE	**238 7/8**	
Percentage of Irregularity	**16.3%**	

'Er Gets Done
Fresh From a Bout of Buck Fever, PA Teen Doesn't Make the Same Mistake Twice
Hanna Harris Buck

Photo courtesy J. Harris family

Sixteen-year-old Hanna Harris would've been positively gleeful if she'd shot the 6-pointer that passed by her deer stand on the morning of Pennsylvania's 2010 rifle opener.

The young buck was hers for the taking, too, but she watched it melt back into the trees without firing a shot. So wracked with buck fever, her jumpy synapses were arcing like downed power lines.

Her trigger finger just didn't get the juice.

That was Hanna's first time to hunt unaccompanied. She was in her mother's elevated stand on the family's 280 acres, alone, though many other Harrises and some friends were loaded for deer elsewhere on the farm.

Opening day is a big deal.

Every year, the Harris's garage in Danville becomes a makeshift camp for orange-clad hunters. Fifteen participated in 2010: Hanna, her parents and two siblings, her Grandpa, a cousin, an uncle and seven more close family friends.

Before heading afield that first morning, everyone drooled over a trail camera photograph of a massive 16-point buck that had been taken just four days earlier. They all wanted a chance at it.

Monday was a perfect day (the rain came Tuesday, and snow fell on Wednesday). It was cold, partly cloudy, and there was only a wisp of wind.

Hanna went to her mom's stand at the edge of a mature oak flat. The open woods were bordered by thick bedding area and a stand of pines. From her vantage point 20 feet aloft, she had a terrific view of the surrounding ground.

Her mother, Maria, had taken at least six bucks from that stand over the years, during both archery and gun seasons.

Hanna carried a Remington Model 700 in .280 caliber, which her dad's cousin gave her.

"He said it was to end the confusion about who was hunting with what gun," Hanna said. "Also, because mom was using a .280, we could share bullets."

Hanna's dad, Joe, walked her to the stand, and then continued on to where he and her little brother were going to sit.

"Even before daylight, I saw two does eating acorns in the flat, so I was too excited to fall asleep, which I tended to do when I was with my dad," Hanna said.

About 7:00, she saw three more deer approaching. One was a doe, one a spike, and the other was a 6-point buck.

"The 6-pointer was bringing up the rear, and when they started getting close, I got really nervous," she said.

"They were going toward the thicket, and I knew I would have to get on the deer quickly if I was going to get a shot.

"I was so nervous, however, that I just couldn't get the gun settled on it, and then they were gone into the brush.

"I was really bummed because I didn't get a shot at that deer," Hanna continued. "I stood there, mad, trying to understand why I was so nervous."

The answer never came, not that she had a lot of time to ponder her inaction.

"While I was thinking, I looked back over to my

left and saw a doe. A few minutes later, another one appeared. Both were walking slowly toward the thicket."

Beyond them was a buck, and Hanna wasted no time in planting a knee against the stand's rail so she would be steadier if she got a chance to shoot. Whatever muddled her brain a few minutes earlier had left with the lucky 6-pointer.

"When this buck stopped behind a double tree, I could see its rack on both sides of the trunks. I knew it was big," she said.

"I couldn't shoot while the buck was behind the tree, but I was right on it, just waiting for it to move. I made sure my safety was off, and I waited.

"When it took two or three steps forward, I was afraid it wouldn't stop, at first. But it did. A few seconds later, after I was sure I was steady, I pulled the trigger," she added.

Hanna lost sight of the buck for a few seconds afterward, but then she saw one of the does run into the pines, and the buck was behind her. The doe ran out the other side. The buck didn't.

"I waited and watched for a few minutes. I didn't see the buck go down, and I didn't see it react to the shot, so I wasn't sure if I'd made a good shot," she said. "Finally, I called my dad. He told me to stay in the stand, and he and Joey would come over and have a look."

Hanna did as instructed, but she couldn't sit. She paced in the platform until her dad and brother arrived, and then she pointed to where the buck went into the pines.

"They started where I shot the deer before walking over to the pines, looking at the ground the whole way," Hanna said. "I didn't know if they were looking at a blood trail, tracks or what, and they weren't telling me anything before they got right to the edge of the pines."

Her father yelled before they entered the pines.

"Okay, Hanna ... You can unload your gun and get down now to have a look!"

Hanna lowered her gun, got down and walked over to her dad and brother.

"My brother started to tease me by saying it was just a little spike buck," she said. "I was handing my gun to my dad when I saw the deer lying just inside the pines.

"It took me like 10 minutes to realize just how big it really was. I counted the points, all 16 of them. It was a huge rack," she continued. "The buck was way bigger than I am.

"We called my mom, who was hunting with Paige, and they also came over to have a look. I called my cousin, Allan, too. He had given me the rifle. When he answered his phone, I just said to him, 'I just shot the biggest buck in the world with this new gun you gave me.'

"My dad and brother walked back to the house to get the ATV, while my mom, sister and I stayed there with the buck. When he returned and loaded it, I drove the four-wheeler back to the house, while they all walked alongside.

"By the time we got home, there was already a crowd waiting to see my buck. Allan said he was very proud of me," Hanna said. "The rest of the day was very exciting as we took pictures and showed it to just about everyone in Danville, and everyone took pictures of me and my buck!"

Photo courtesy J. Harris family

Hanna Harris Buck

Official Buckmasters Score Sheet		
Taken by:	**Hanna Harris**	
Date:	**November 29, 2010**	
Location:	**Northumberland Co, Pa.**	
Method:	**Modern Rifle**	
Classification:	**Semi-Irregular**	
Measurements:	**Right**	**Left**
Total Points Side	**8**	**8**
Irregular Points Side	**3**	**3**
Total Irregular Inches	**6 3/8**	**8 4/8**
Length of Main Beam	**27 5/8**	**27 1/8**
Length of 1st Point	**7 3/8**	**6 1/8**
Length of 2nd Point	**9 5/8**	**9 1/8**
Length of 3rd Point	**12 2/8**	**12 2/8**
Length of 4th Point	**10**	**9 4/8**
Length of 5th Point		
Length of 6th Point		
1st Circumference (C1)	**5 2/8**	**5 2/8**
2nd Circumference (C2)	**4 6/8**	**5 5/8**
3rd Circumference (C3)	**4 6/8**	**5 5/8**
4th Circumference (C4)	**5 2/8**	**6**
Score Per Side	**93 2/8**	**95 1/8**
OFFICIAL SCORE	**188 3/8**	
Inside Spread	**20 7/8**	
COMPOSITE SCORE	**209 2/8**	
Percentage of Irregularity	**7.8%**	

Buck in the Burbs
Scott Esker Buck

Photo courtesy Scott Esker

Scott Esker and his twin brother, Steve, hunt seven days a week, 52 weeks a year. When not carrying a bow, they're packing a camera.

"We scout every day as we go about our jobs, and every evening throughout the spring, summer, fall and winter," Scott says. "We are always looking for new places to hunt and taking care of the places we already have. We are definitely dedicated, maybe addicted to it. And we hunt urban deer almost exclusively."

Scott sells new houses for Trinity/Ambassador Homes in a large Midwestern city. His familiarity with all of the properties he handles and the new homeowners he closes help him professionally and as a deer hunter.

"I try to be good friends with all the homeowners in our developments. It is good for business, and it has fringe benefits you cannot buy," says Scott.

He was sitting in the office one day in November 2008 when he got a call from one of his homeowners with questions about refinancing. But before delving into interest rates, she told Scott that she and her husband had been seeing a huge buck in their back yard for two or three days at about the same time – 10:30. She also asked if he would like to see a photograph of it, which she offered to e-mail.

"A few hours later, I opened the e-mail and saw a monstrous buck standing in a field. I drooled," Scott said. "What an incredible rack on that monster … at least five long tines on each side, plus double brow tines and more … much more!

"I was excited because I knew I could hunt

behind where those folks live. My brother and I had scouted that area many times. There always was lots of great deer sign, but we had no inkling that this fellow lived in the neighborhood," he continued.

"I called the woman right back," Scott said. "I was skeptical, at first; almost sure it must be a joke. I even tried to get her to admit that she had copied the photo from a magazine just to get me going. But she said, 'No, I have the pictures on my camera right now.' So I asked could I come over to have a look.

"She said, 'Yes, come on over and I'll show them to you.'"

Scott went over to their house the very next morning, pretty much stopping everything else he was doing. Already familiar with the property, when Scott arrived he stood to the side of their home and surveyed the large field that borders their property on two sides. It was an immense section of his company's property that had not yet been developed.

It consisted of a large fallow field, overgrown with ragweed, goldenrod and every other weed that grows, and farther back a tree line at the border. To the distant left was an apartment complex; to the right, another housing development. After a good look, Scott went to the door and rang the bell.

He was ushered into the home and soon began a serious inquisition of the owners. All doubts were erased when the camera was produced.

"I turned it on and started to scroll through the pictures. There stood the buck, just off to the side of their property. I was able to recognize several distinct landmarks," he said. "No doubt: The pictures were genuine, and I was in awe!

"I asked them if they minded if I set up a ground blind just beyond their privacy fence and tried to take this deer," he continued. "They told me I was very welcome to do that. It had been one of the reasons they had called me in the first place!"

Scott's ground blind, however, was on another piece of ground several miles away. And he didn't really want to move it. After a quick survey of the area behind the fence, Scott picked out a spot in the field next to the lone tree on the other side of the fence. He would use it to help break up his silhouette and build some kind of a blind.

Hurrying home, Scott surveyed the contents of his garage. In one corner lay the remnants of his wedding reception: beach stuff, including several hula skirts. He decided they would be just the right color to match the dried weeds in the field. Several of them, tied between metal fence posts, should provide adequate cover. So Scott hastily grabbed them and headed back to the ambush site.

He quickly set up his makeshift blind and readied it for the afternoon hunt. He then returned home to shower and suit up for the evening. Once back in position, he set up his buck decoy along a cleared shooting lane and got out his rattling antlers.

After a short rattling session, he scanned the field with his binoculars. He also realized that his perfect ambush site was on low ground. He could see only a small portion of the field. The ground next to the fence, 20 yards away, was at least 4 or 5 feet higher. Curious, he quickly made his way to the fence so he could peek over and see the rest of the field.

After a quick consultation with the homeowner, Scott moved his "hula blind" to higher ground right behind the privacy fence, and he cut another shooting lane through the 4- to 5-foot-tall weeds. But that presented another problem.

Being up against the fence meant he could no longer survey the right side of the field because he couldn't see through or over the barrier to where the buck had been photographed.

The issue was resolved when he borrowed a small four-step ladder to lean against the fence. He had high hopes for the following morning.

"I was worked up all night about my setup," he said. "As soon as I awoke, I showered and dressed in my Scent-Lok clothing. When I arrived, I knew I had to sneak around the fence and get in place without disturbing any deer that might be in the field beyond," said Scott. "I moved down to the end of the fence and slowly peered around the corner to see a small 8-point buck, so I hunkered down at the end of the fence and waited for it to leave.

"As soon as it disappeared, I hurried over to the blind, set up my decoy and waited for daylight. I rattled as soon as dawn broke, glassed the field continuously for 30 minutes, and then did another sequence.

"Seeing nothing, I stepped up on the ladder to peer over the fence. Even without binoculars, I could see the huge buck about 200 yards away and coming toward me. But it stopped at 70 yards.

"The buck started milling around the middle of

the field at that point," he continued. "I eased down and picked up my video camera to film the buck, but I was anything but calm. My heart was pounding, and I was shaking. There it was, right in front of me, but no longer interested in heading my way. Rattling and grunting were having no effect, and I was perplexed.

"I needed to talk to someone, to get my mind settled down and to soothe my nerves," Scott said. "So I called my brother, who was sitting in a treestand about half a mile away."

Steve Esker answered his phone, hoping to hear that Scott had tagged the buck. He was surprised when his brother told him he was looking at it from 70 yards.

"Steve could tell I was nervous," Scott said.

"Calm down now," Steve warned. "Stop rattling and just watch. The buck's too close now anyway. Have you tried grunting?"

"Yes, but nothing seems to be working. Wait … I haven't tried a doe bleat yet. Maybe I should try that?"

"Yeah, that's it. Try the bleat."

"I pulled the call from my gear bag and gave it a try while my brother was still on the telephone," Scott said. "And that did it. Suddenly, the buck was coming in my direction. I whispered into the phone, 'Gotta go … It's coming my way now!'"

Scott grabbed his bow and prepared for the shot he was convinced was moments away.

"I crouched low in the blind and attached my release. I just had to remain calm until it showed up in my lane," he said.

"I waited for what seemed like hours, but

nothing. My legs were starting to burn from squatting. My nerves were tingling. 'Where is it?' I wondered. 'Did it wind me? Has something else happened to spook the deer?'

"I was sorely tempted to stand, step up on the ladder and take a look, but my experience told me not to do that," he added. "I was going crazy with worry. I finally decided I just had to take a look, and as I started to rise up, there it was, almost in my shooting lane.

"I didn't have time to think. I was still squatting when I drew. The buck was less than 5 feet from my shooting lane before it saw the decoy. At 17 yards, it turned and began quartering away from me. I rose, placed the pin on the last rib and released the arrow."

Scott watched as the immense whitetail rocketed away, heading for deep cover. He even stepped up on the ladder.

"At about 100 yards, I watched the giant tip over beside a small tree. I zeroed in on the spot intently, hoping it was down for good," he said. "In my mind, I kept repeating, 'He never got back up. He never got back up.' I was ecstatic!"

That's when he noticed the buck's girlfriend and realized that the doe must have been the cause for its hanging up in the middle of the field.

Not wanting to rush things, Scott sought even higher ground so he could perhaps see his buck on the ground. Before long, he was beyond the fence and standing on the sidewalk in front of his friends' house. But the weeds in the field were too tall to allow a glimpse of the deer.

Scott almost melted onto the ground, mentally

exhausted, physically drained and simply tired from a sleepless night. He lay down and called his wife to share the news. He also called his brother, who said, "Hold tight until I get there."

While all this was happening, a neighbor saw the strange man in full camo lying on the sidewalk across from her house. She dialed 911 to report the unusual situation.

Meanwhile, Scott got up and went over to sit on the porch of his friends' house to wait for his brother.

Within minutes, Scott was startled when a police car pulled up and stopped on the street in front of him. Scott rose from his seat, waved to and approached the officer. The policeman asked what he was doing, and Scott told him he'd been bowhunting behind the house, had just shot a monster buck and was waiting for his brother to arrive to help find it. The police officer was cool, obviously familiar with urban hunters and not the least alarmed with Scott's demeanor.

"We talked for several minutes. I told him about the deer and that I was cooling off while the deer expired," Scott said. He asked if I had permission to hunt here, and I told him I had the paperwork in my truck, and he asked to see it. I showed him the permission papers, and he was satisfied. After that, he went across the street to assure the lady that everything was okay."

Steve arrived soon afterward, and they went straight to where Scott saw the buck fall. Sure enough, it was lying right there. Once they found the deer, they asked the officer if he wanted to come down and see it.

All three men exchanged high-fives.

While they were standing there, the cop got a radio call from another officer checking on him. Within minutes, a second police car pulled up to the curb. Two more cruisers arrived a short while later.

It got even more exciting when a team from Wolf Creek Productions heard about the harvest and arrived on the scene with their cameras rolling. Steve knew they were in the area trying to film a hunt, so he called them.

Photo courtesy Scott Esker

Scott Esker Buck

Official Buckmasters Score Sheet		
Taken by:	**Scott Esker**	
Date:	**November 14, 2008**	
Location:	**Fairfield Co., Ohio**	
Method:	**Compound Bow**	
Classification:	**Irregular**	
Measurements:	**Right**	**Left**
Total Points Side	12	11
Irregular Points Side	6	5
Total Irregular Inches	18 1/8	10 4/8
Length of Main Beam	28 5/8	29 1/8
Length of 1st Point	9 3/8	5 5/8
Length of 2nd Point	11 3/8	10 7/8
Length of 3rd Point	11	11 3/8
Length of 4th Point	9 4/8	8 7/8
Length of 5th Point	1 1/8	3 7/8
Length of 6th Point		
1st Circumference (C1)	5 6/8	5 6/8
2nd Circumference (C2)	5 3/8	5 5/8
3rd Circumference (C3)	5 1/8	5 1/8
4th Circumference (C4)	5 1/8	4 5/8
Score Per Side	110 4/8	101 3/8
OFFICIAL SCORE	211 7/8	
Inside Spread	24	
COMPOSITE SCORE	235 7/8	
Percentage of Irregularity	13.5%	

Whizz Kid
When ya gotta go, ya gotta go!
Joseph Bradley Buck

Photo courtesy Joe Bradley

Joe Bradley's dogged determination to stick with the same stand was wavering. The hunter from Springfield, Ohio, had sat in the exact spot three days in a row without seeing a single deer. But at least he hadn't spooked any, he hoped.

"I was convinced that it was a good stand location, and I knew there were loads of deer on the Clark County farm," Joe said. "I also knew that there was (or at least had been) a big buck in the area."

During the previous, 1998 bow season, Joe discovered a very large rub on a 6-inch diameter oak tree in a fencerow not far from the woodlot that he was watching a year later.

Joe couldn't understand why he wasn't at least seeing some does. It was Nov. 5, within a week of the rut's peak.

Big rubs aside, he'd chosen to set up there because he could watch a trail in front of the stand that ran north to south, from a bedding directly to a feeding area. A second, heavily used trail from the east intersected the main corridor right in front of his stand. Both trails were being used regularly by the neighborhood whitetails.

This was to be his last day to stand guard there.

"I decided that I would hunt it one more time," Joe said. "I put some doe-in-heat scent on pads tied to the bottoms of my boots, and I walked down the corn field, alongside the woodlot to the east. I then turned into the woods and followed the east-west trail all the way to the treestand.

Before climbing into it, I also walked the north-south trail close to the bedding area, all the while (hopefully) leaving a good scent trail back to my stand.

"I also hung a scented rag in a tree near the bedding area, and then I went back and settled in my stand," Joe continued.

Still, despite his well-laid plan, four long and uneventful hours passed. Then his bladder started sending him signals.

"It was just about sunset, and I had to go bad," Joe grinned. "I thought if I crawled out of this tree, I'll never get back up here again in time to do any good. The wind just happened to be blowing right across the trail, but —since that was my last time to hunt there — I stood up and answered the call.

"About 15 minutes later, here comes the buck, right up the trail from the east, head down as it was sniffing the scent that I'd laid. I could not shoot because the deer was on the left, so I had to go around the other side of the tree.

"I shot him left-handed as he passed almost underneath me. I got him right down through the ribs from the top," Joe beamed.

"The crossbow's bolt entered about two, no, three inches, well maybe four inches to the right of the spine and penetrated to the fletching. I didn't even see the buck flinch. It just continued on toward the bedding area.

"I just sat there and watched the deer walk off, knowing that it was a good hit because I could see the arrow. I eventually lost sight of him in the brush, but then I heard a cough and saw antlers move within the bedding area about 50 yards‘ away, and then there was silence," he said.

After a few minutes, Joe could not wait any longer. He got down from the tree and walked toward the bedding area, where the buck was lying.

"He was huge," Joe exclaimed. "I could not even move him; he was too big!"

Joe is very glad that the buck did not travel far, because there was not even a drop of blood to follow.

As he stood there in the dark, unable to budge the giant whitetail, which weighed more than 300 pounds, Joe decided to go ahead and field dress it. Afterward, he covered it for safe-keeping and headed for home.

"I couldn't leave it there overnight because there are too many coyotes in the area, and I did not want to risk losing the meat or the trophy," he said. "When I got home, I called the fellow that was farming the land and persuaded him to come out with a front-loader. We went right into the woods, loaded it in the front-loader and hauled it out to my truck."

When Joe saw that buck coming down the trail, he knew it was something special. From the time he first saw the buck until it disappeared from sight, no more than two minutes could have elapsed.

"I really didn't have time to get nervous or flustered, so I just concentrated on getting a clean shot," Joe said.

Photo courtesy Joe Bradley

Joseph Bradley Buck

Official Buckmasters Score Sheet		
Taken by:	**Joseph Bradley**	
Date:	**November 13, 2000**	
Location:	**Clark Co., Ohio**	
Method:	**Crossbow**	
Classification:	**Perfect**	
Measurements:	**Right**	Left
Total Points Side	5	5
Irregular Points Side	0	0
Total Irregular Inches	0	0
Length of Main Beam	22	21 6/8
Length of 1st Point	7 1/8	9 2/8
Length of 2nd Point	9	10 3/8
Length of 3rd Point	9 6/8	9 4/8
Length of 4th Point	6 1/8	6
Length of 5th Point		
Length of 6th Point		
1st Circumference (C1)	4 4/8	4 4/8
2nd Circumference (C2)	4 4/8	4 4/8
3rd Circumference (C3)	4 4/8	4 6/8
4th Circumference (C4)	4 2/8	4 6/8
Score Per Side	71 6/8	75 3/8
OFFICIAL SCORE	147 1/8	
Inside Spread	16 3/8	
COMPOSITE SCORE	163 4/8	
Percentage of Irregularity	0.0%	

In Praise of Point-and-Shoots
Greg Deckling Buck

Photo courtesy Greg Deckling

Greg Deckling, like most bowhunters, realizes the importance of practice. If you can't launch at least a few arrows prior to opening day, there's really no point in going.

Even if the sights are dead-on, it takes a little conditioning to be able to draw and hold a compound bow. The college junior has no place on campus to shoot his bow. But because he lives in Ohio, where crossbows and red-dot sights aren't restricted to the aged and infirm, the lack of practice didn't keep him out of the woods when the season opened last year.

So they'd be able to hunt together, Bill Deckling offered to let his son use a crossbow that had belonged to a friend who'd lost his battle with lung cancer the previous December.

Even so, Greg missed the morning hunt.

"Dad and I were in the garage about 5 a.m., loading all our gear and going over our checklist," Greg said. "As Dad ticked things off, he said 'deer tag,' and I stopped what I was doing. I'd forgotten to get mine.

"He told me, 'Well, you might as well go back to bed then, because you can't go hunting without it,'" he continued.

Later, when the local shops were open, Greg bought his deer tag so he could hunt that evening. He was excited at the prospect of encountering one of the several nice bucks his father had seen prior to the season.

"My neighbor and I started scouting about the middle of July, driving the back roads and glassing the edges of fields," Bill said. "One afternoon, we saw three decent bucks in a bean field near the property we hunt.

"Two of the bucks had pretty nice racks, but that third one was huge. It was hard to tell exactly because of the velvet, but I thought it might have a third beam. My neighbor thought it could be a drop tine.

"I immediately started putting out trail cameras in hopes of catching some close-ups," Greg's dad continued. "I put bucket loads of apples in an area where I hoped we could easily draw them."

Bill started getting photographs of the wonky deer on July 31. It seemed both he and his pal were right. Not only was there an extra beam, but there was also a drop tine.

They continued baiting three trail cam stations, and Bill kept Greg abreast of the deer's comings and goings.

"I told Greg that if he wanted a chance at the biggest of the bucks that were frequenting the area around his stand, including the triple-beamed one, he would need to get down here for opening day," Bill said.

Well, at least half a day was better than missing the whole opening act. With a fresh license in his wallet, Greg joined his dad that afternoon.

Their stands were about 100 yards apart.

To break the monotony, Bill eventually texted his son, asking if he knew the Ohio State football score. After being updated, he settled back into the peace and quiet.

"About 6:45, my phone vibrated. It was Greg, and I thought he might be calling to tell me the final score," Bill said. "The instant I answered, he shouted, 'Dad, I got him! I got the big one!' All I could say was, 'No you didn't!'"

But Greg persisted, and Bill got down from his stand and soon joined his son.

"I hadn't seen much of anything other than squirrels all afternoon, but around 5:45 or so, I saw some brown in the trees to my right," Greg said. "It was a very nice 9-pointer we had seen on the trail cameras, but I had no shot at it.

"About 6:40, I heard what sounded like a deer running through the cornfield behind my stand. I didn't see anything, at first," he continued. "I was wondering what the noise had been and where the deer, if it was a deer, had gone.

"Suddenly, a slight movement caused me to look almost straight down at this huge buck. It was standing only 6 or 7 yards away, looking up at me," he said.

Greg couldn't move, and the crossbow was lying in his lap. But then he remembered the red dot scope.

"I very carefully turned it on while the buck was looking at me," he said. "In slow-motion, I swung the bow around and pointed it downward, trying to get the red dot centered for a shot, but it wasn't bright enough for me to see it.

"It seemed like hours passed before I finally got the intensity bright enough to see it on the ground. Still, I couldn't bring the crossbow around far enough to aim," Greg continued. "I remember thinking, *I don't have a chance*."

Fortunately for Greg, a piece of corn stalk was tangled in the buck's antlers, which must have been interfering with its view of the blob in the tree.

"When the deer suddenly lowered its head and started shaking the stalk out of its antlers, that gave me the chance to bring the bow fully around, though still in my lap," Greg said. "I raised the red dot to the buck's shoulder and tripped the trigger."

Greg saw the bolt strike the buck, which jumped and ran about 15 yards out into an alfalfa field. It stood there for a several seconds before trotting over and disappearing into the opposite tree line, and that's when Greg called his father.

"I was pretty excited. I didn't even think about being quiet anymore. I just wanted to tell someone what had happened," he said.

Bill told Greg to stay in his stand. When he got there, his son directed him to the arrow sticking in the ground. There was plenty of blood, but Bill didn't like the color.

"We found only a few spots of blood in the alfalfa field," he said. "Convinced we were in for a long and difficult search, I called my brother, Steve, who is the best tracker I know. I wanted to 'get him moving in our direction before dark."

Steve, however, was attending a wedding, which meant the two of them would have to forge ahead, fingers crossed.

A little farther, they came across a pool of red stuff. There was even more where the deer entered the woods.

"I had thought about backing off, but after seeing all that new sign, I felt pretty sure we'd find the deer," Bill said.

The trail led father and son into a CRP field. About 20 yards into it, they found the buck.

"I just know old Tom — the bow's former owner — was watching over my shoulder that day," Greg said. "If it hadn't been for that red dot scope and the corn stalk in the buck's antlers, I never would've been able to shoot!"

Photo courtesy Greg Deckling

Greg Deckling Buck

Official Buckmasters Score Sheet		
Taken by:	**Greg Deckling**	
Date:	**September 29, 2012**	
Location:	**Morrow Co., Ohio**	
Method:	**Crossbow**	
Classification:	**Irregular**	
Measurements:	**Right**	**Left**
Total Points Side	**13**	**8**
Irregular Points Side	**8**	**2**
Total Irregular Inches	**57 6/8**	**5 1/8**
Length of Main Beam	**22 1/8**	**24 7/8**
Length of 1st Point	**5 6/8**	**4 5/8**
Length of 2nd Point	**6**	**7 5/8**
Length of 3rd Point	**6 4/8**	**10**
Length of 4th Point	**4**	**9 5/8**
Length of 5th Point		**3 7/8**
Length of 6th Point		
1st Circumference (C1)	**3 6/8**	**4 6/8**
2nd Circumference (C2)	**4 1/8**	**4 3/8**
3rd Circumference (C3)	**4**	**4 5/8**
4th Circumference (C4)	**3 5/8**	**4 6/8**
Score Per Side	**117 5/8**	**84 2/8**
OFFICIAL SCORE	**201 7/8**	
Inside Spread	**20 3/8**	
COMPOSITE SCORE	**222 2/8**	
Percentage of Irregularity	**31.1%**	

CRASH COURSE
Alisha Perkins Buck

Photo courtesy of Alisha Perkins

Convincing herself that accompanying her husband in a deer stand might be the only way she could enjoy a cheap, long overdue and child-free outing with her beloved, Alisha Perkins agreed last year to take a crash course in hunting.

She had no idea it would wind up costing far more than dinner for two at a swanky restaurant. And he had no idea their date would end in tears.

Neither, however, have any regrets.

"My husband, Seth, shot a buck on opening day of Ohio's 2012 archery season," Alisha said. "He filled his doe tag a few days later.

"His family owns and operates Whitefeather Meats in Creston, so he processes all of his deer at home," she added. "Both his deer were already in the freezer when this huge buck made its first appearance on one of his trail cameras."

The nighttime photo was taken Oct. 27 at one of their farms in Summit County. The buck was " clearly in a league of its own, which is why Seth decided to recruit his wife.

"When we married, I knew Seth had a passion for bowhunting. I also knew that, at some point, I would have to decide whether to join him or to become a hunter's widow for four months of every year," Alisha said.

Having and raising two young sons delayed that, until last fall. "I had never hunted, and I wasn't sure I was ready," she admitted. "But the buck in the photo was beautiful and Seth and his dad were both done for the year."

In order for the Perkins men to hunt vicariously through her, Alisha had to immediately take and pass the required hunter safety course, which she did, and with flying colors. Buying her first license came next, and then they had to find some clothes that would fit, as well as a suitable weapon.

"My father-in-law was more than happy to loan' me his crossbow, so, on Friday afternoon, Seth and I went over there for my first shooting lessons," she said. "Afterward, we got up on the roof of the house to pretend we were in a stand. I shot as various distances, and I hit the bull's-eye each time. It was really quite easy. I had no idea crossbows could be so accurate."

At 5:00 the next morning, Nov. 10, Seth's parents arrived to babysit 4 year-old Luke and 2-year-old Logan. It was raining when Seth and Alisha departed for the farm.

"We entered the woods and made our way to a double ladder stand near where the camera had taken the picture of the buck," Alisha said. "I was wearing some kind of snow pants that swished with every step I took. I couldn't help it, but Seth was giving me the evil eye, especially after we busted some deer.

"We climbed into the stand about 6:30, just as the rain stopped. I was quite nervous. I had never shot anything in my entire life, not a rabbit, squirrel or even a bird.

"It was so foreign to me," she said.

When they settled in to wait, they realized that Alisha, a right-handed shooter, was sitting on the left side. So they swapped positions. Once situated, Seth said a prayer.

"Seth eventually saw a doe off in the distance, slowly coming our way. He kept trying to point it out to me, but I couldn't see anything," Alisha said. "The more I looked, the less I saw, until, finally, I looked down and saw the deer almost underneath us, eating acorns and occasionally rubbing the top of its head. Seth thought it was a button buck.

"I asked if he wanted me to shoot it, since I am not one of those people fascinated by bone on the top of a deer's head," she continued.

I said, "I can go ahead and take the shot if you want me to," but Seth thought it was too early. The rut was starting, and things were going well for us.

"We watched the button buck for almost half an hour," Alisha said. "Later, I heard what sounded like Godzilla coming through woods. Turns out, it was just squirrels. I didn't know how quiet deer are when they walk."

Alisha eventually spotted movement and squinted to see a large buck approaching. She immediately took the safety off and got ready to shoot.

"I had never hunted before, but I sure had watched lots of hunting shows over the years. I knew what an ethical shot was (not a head-on one), and I didn't want to make a bad one," she said. "I'd also gotten a good lecture about all those things in the truck that morning.

"The buck came straight in, never offering more than a head-on shot. It stood in front of us for 10 minutes, 40 seconds, according to my husband. When it finally started walking away, I took my eyes off the crosshairs and looked at Seth. I didn't know if I should take a shot at a moving animal."

Seth did a bleat thing with his mouth, and the buck stopped, broadside to us," she said. "It took a few seconds for me to settle the crosshairs and pull the trigger."

The deer went down immediately, got back up, and then staggered to the left before falling again. "I started crying," Alisha said. "My first words were: 'Oh my gosh! I'm sorry. I'm so sorry I did that!'

"It was very traumatic for me," she added. "I don't know if I can ever do it again.

"I decided to view the whole experience like a cheap date night, since we never get away from the kids otherwise. It was a great experience for us to share," Alisha said.

It wound up not being so cheap, though, because of the taxidermy bill. Not that she's complaining. "Never in a million years would I have thought I'd end up in the woods shooting things. I still can't believe it."

"Although this buck will be hard to top, I

probably will do it again. I'm definitely looking forward to taking the boys when they are of age," she added.

Alisha Perkins Buck

Official Buckmasters Score Sheet		
Taken by:	**Alisha Perkins**	
Date:	**November 10, 2012**	
Location:	**Summit Co., Ohio**	
Method:	**Crossbow**	
Classification:	**Irregular**	
Measurements:	**Right**	Left
Total Points Side	8	10
Irregular Points Side	4	6
Total Irregular Inches	18 6/8	15 4/8
Length of Main Beam	28	28 2/8
Length of 1st Point	4 7/8	3 1/8
Length of 2nd Point	10 2/8	11
Length of 3rd Point	6 4/8	8 2/8
Length of 4th Point		1 3/8
Length of 5th Point		
Length of 6th Point		
1st Circumference (C1)	4 7/8	5
2nd Circumference (C2)	4 6/8	4 4/8
3rd Circumference (C3)	6 1/8	4 5/8
4th Circumference (C4)	4 4/8	4 3/8
Score Per Side	88 5/8	86
OFFICIAL SCORE	174 5/8	
Inside Spread	20 5/8	
COMPOSITE SCORE	195 2/8	
Percentage of Irregularity	19.6%	

UNBEKNOWNST
Carl Morris Buck

Photo courtesy Ed Waite

Buddies Carl Morris Jr. and Jeremy Martin were convinced that the bull of their woods was a photogenic 12-pointer with a gleaming white rack. Of the many deer their trail cameras photographed during the weeks leading up to Ohio's 2011 season, the big 6X6 stood out like a Brahma in a goat pen.

Understandably, that buck was at the top of their wish lists. Not a day passed when at least one — if not both — of them was in a stand, hoping to see the behemoth within an arrow's reach.

The guys have permission to hunt a 100-acre farm in Licking County, which they typically begin scouting in August. Carl, who owns a landscaping business near Columbus, says even though they've hunted the place for several years, they still like to see what might await them.

"The trail cams help us see what kind of deer pass through there," he said. "The best, hands-down, was this beautiful 12-pointer. Its antlers were almost pure white, like they had been polished. There was no mistaking it in the photos."

Carl and Jeremy had four stands on the place.

"The one I refer to as Jeremy's stand overlooks the edge of a cornfield," Carl explained. "I have one close to there, in the middle of the woods that covers the trail leading to the field."

Those two setups beckoned Carl on Nov. 4. Jeremy was out of town that day.

"The afternoon was quite nice with a slight northwest wind and temperature of nearly 50 degrees," he said. "Since Jeremy was up in northern Ohio and would not get back in time because of the traffic, I decided to sit his stand. I had been seeing a group of deer about 100 yards from my setup and closer to his

"Since the farmer had cut the corn the previous week, the stubble had become a deer buffet," Carl continued. "We had been hunting pretty much all week and had seen quite a few deer."

Carl arrived home that Friday later than he'd hoped. By the time he changed clothes, drove out to the farm and climbed into his friend's stand with his crossbow, there was only about an hour of shooting light remaining.

Turns out, that was all he needed.

"I had been in the stand for only a short time when a big doe came walking toward me about 6:15. She kept looking over her shoulder, too, so I knew something was behind her," he said.

"I finally saw the buck exiting the trees, and my heart started pounding. It was not the 12-pointer I'd been hoping all season to see. This guy was a total stranger. We had no idea a deer of that caliber was out there!

"From about 75 yards out, it eventually wound up behind me," he continued. "I was not able to get a shot, but my eyes were riveted on the deer.

"Fortunately for me, the doe circled back toward me, and the buck followed her. When it was about 50 yards out, I raised my crossbow," Carl said.

"I was just about ready to shoot when the buck suddenly turned and bounced off about 50 yards. I was sure I had missed my opportunity.

"With the buck standing there, I tried my grunt call. But the deer moved even farther away from me. When I grunted again, the doe made a move and, once again, her boyfriend started coming closer, hugging cover," he added.

The buck came to within 20 yards that time, but Carl still had no shot through the brush. When it turned and started walking away from him, the hunter in the tree tasted bile.

"My nerves were shot," he said. "So close, but yet so far."

When the deer had backed off about 40 yards, Carl heard someone start and take off on a four-wheeler. The buck heard it, too, and raised its head to look in the direction of the noise.

Then, to Carl's surprise, rather than walk away from the noise, the buck started walking toward it, which meant it was coming back!

"The deer came directly underneath my stand. I could neither shoot nor breathe," he said. "It stood there for forever, or 50 seconds, whichever is longer, and then turned around and started walking away once more.

"That time, I had a shot. It was only 10 yards away when I squeezed the trigger. Afterward, the buck ran about 40 yards, stopped and looked back at me. After a short pause, it started walking away as if nothing had happened.

"It re-entered the woods about 100 yards distant," he added. Because nightfall was just a few minutes away, Carl remained seated and called Jeremy, who had made it home.

"Jeremy and I checked the spot where I connected and found the arrow and lots of blood. After marking the spot, we headed for the house to eat and to collect our tracking gear. We went back out at 11 p.m.," he said.

"The farther we went, the more nervous I got. After 100 yards, the blood trail became sparse. By the time we had covered the second 100 yards, we were really straining to find the next drops.

"We eventually walked the entire length of the woods, more than 500 yards. The buck seemed to have traveled a straight line toward another cornfield.

"Upon reaching the field, we were both pretty depressed. We had searched for hours," Carl said.

With wide open space in front of them, Jeremy pointed his powerful flashlight into the corn stubble to scan the field. Seeing the buck's enormous white belly was the anti- depressant the pals needed.

"After some serious handshaking and back-slapping, we admired the incredible buck. It was bigger than I'd thought," Carl said.

"Jeremy was dumbfounded. So was I," he added. "We had no idea this buck existed."

Later, when they examined the buck under the glare of garage lights, they discovered Carl's shot had been perfect; the bolt had double-lunged the animal. That it still managed to run 600 yards is both amazing and testament to a Whitetail's stamina.

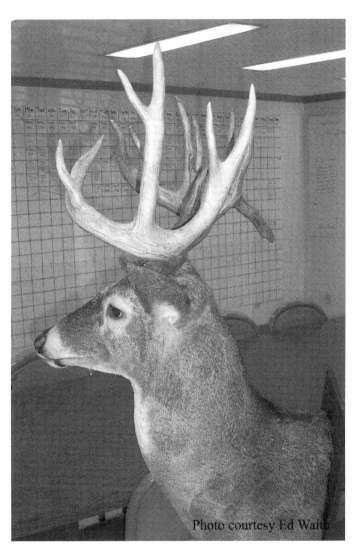

Photo courtesy Ed Waite

Carl Morris Buck

Official Buckmasters Score Sheet		
Taken by:	**Carl Morris**	
Date:	**November 4, 2011**	
Location:	**Licking Co., Ohio**	
Method:	**Crossbow**	
Classification:	**Irregular**	
Measurements:	**Right**	**Left**
Total Points Side	**10**	**7**
Irregular Points Side	**5**	**2**
Total Irregular Inches	**23 3/8**	**8 2/8**
Length of Main Beam	**25 4/8**	**24 3/8**
Length of 1st Point	**6 3/8**	**6 7/8**
Length of 2nd Point	**10 3/8**	**10 6/8**
Length of 3rd Point	**9 5/8**	**11 7/8**
Length of 4th Point	**5 3/8**	**5**
Length of 5th Point		
Length of 6th Point		
1st Circumference (C1)	**5 6/8**	**5 4/8**
2nd Circumference (C2)	**4 4/8**	**4 5/8**
3rd Circumference (C3)	**5**	**5 4/8**
4th Circumference (C4)	**4 2/8**	**4**
Score Per Side	**100 1/8**	**86 6/8**
OFFICIAL SCORE	**186 7/8**	
Inside Spread	**18 2/8**	
COMPOSITE SCORE	**205 1/8**	
Percentage of Irregularity	**16.9%**	

On a Whim
Jim Twiggs Buck

Photo supplied by Jim Twiggs

After spending most of Oct. 7, 2012, cutting up fallen trees, dragging the debris to the woods and decommissioning a storm-damaged stand, most hunters would've been happy to spend the remains of the day in a recliner.

Jim Twiggs might've done just that, too, if his buddy hadn't announced that he was going to see the sunset from a deer stand. Once that notion was planted, it germinated in all of three seconds.

Jim's friend, Ted Galbreath, had brought his hunting gear to the farm, so staying to hunt was an easy choice. Jim, however, had to go home to collect his stuff, and then drive back in order to sit in a tree for a couple of hours.

"Since we had been working on one side of the farm, making lots of noise, we decided to hunt the other side," Jim said. "The stand I chose was in a wooded strip beside a stream. I'd re-hung it that morning."

The trees flanking the waterway are just about the only cover on the 300-plus-acre farm, which is next to a very large tract that's off-limits to hunters. Jim's stand was closest to a hay field, though there was corn stubble to the north and cut soybeans to the south.

He'd shot a nice 9-pointer from there the previous season. "I was in it by 5:00," he said. "Ten minutes later, a small doe came to drink from the stream. She then ventured out into the alfalfa and began feeding. About 50 minutes after she appeared, three more does came in from my left and joined her. They were followed by a little 4-pointer.

"The weather was changing, and the deer were really moving," he added.

Jim was surprised at all the activity. Although he'd hunted the farm for many years, he'd never been afield during the season's first two weeks. Soon, four more small bucks — a 10-pointer, a 6 and a couple more forkhorns — entered the field from the strip of trees behind him. They all walked right past him.

"I was grateful that I was wearing my scent-free clothing," he said.

Most of the deer in the alfalfa had wandered off by 6:30, when another small doe came within 25 yards of Jim's hiding place. After about 15 minutes of quietly feeding, she suddenly jerked up her head and stared at something to Jim's right.

"She immediately bolted and flew past me," he said. "I thought a coyote might be entering the field, but then I spotted a really nice 9-pointer that, judging from its course, would walk past me at 20 yards or so. I was debating whether to take a shot.

"As I toyed with the idea, I spotted more movement out of the corner of my right eye. I slowly turned to see another deer coming through the corner of the field," he continued. "I could make out only four uprights on the left side as it was coming to me, but I could tell the rack also carried very good mass."

He guessed the newcomer was a 10-pointer, and he forgot about the 5X4 he'd been tracking.

"It looked as if it was going to parallel the path the 9-pointer had taken, about 15 to 20 yards farther out in the field," Jim said. "That meant I'd have a 40-yard shot."

Maybe 20 seconds after Jim resolved to take the shot, the buck obliged and crossed in front of him at a brisk pace. After slowing it by Whistling, Jim squeezed his crossbow's trigger.

It looked like the arrow struck the quartering deer's last rib, angled forward, and then passed completely through the animal. Jim could only hope the bolt had pierced the bellows before exiting.

"Both bucks took off running along the field's edge, and then cut through a gap in the trees. I couldn't tell whether one or both went out the other side," Jim said.

"I sat in the stand for another 50 minutes before I got down to look for my arrow, which was black. I wished it had been any other color, because I never found it.

"With no arrow and no trail to follow, I walked toward the cut. It was about 7:50 and starting to get dark," he said. "I dug through my pack and found a pen light, which seemed totally inadequate.

"When I reached the gap, there was blood on both sides of the trail," Jim continued. "That really brightened my outlook."

Hope renewed, he hung his hat on a limb and walked back to his truck to call Ted.

"After Ted arrived, we walked back to the stand so I could show him where the deer had been when I took the shot and where it headed afterward. We then crossed the creek and entered the corn stubble," Jim said. "Soon, my (better) flashlight's beam illuminated the deer's belly.

"The left side of the antlers was sticking up, but the right side was partially buried in the soft earth. I had to pull really hard to free it from the corn stalks and dirt," he said. "Only then did I realize the buck was far more than a decent 10-pointer!

"It had to weigh more than 300 pounds as well," Jim added. "We'd never seen such a buck on that farm."

After exchanging high-fives and hugging, the men realized that four arms and legs might not be enough to load the antlered boxcar, so they called Ted's son, who lived -nearby. He brought three other guys as reinforcements.

James also called the landowner to explain the soon-to-arrive traffic, and the man came out to see the buck as well.

"The next morning, I took the deer to Bob Anderson's taxidermy shop and hung it in his cooler," he said.

Photo supplied by Jim Twiggs

Jim Twiggs Buck

Official Buckmasters Score Sheet		
Taken by:	**Jim Twiggs**	
Date:	**October 7, 2012**	
Location:	**Clark Co., Ohio**	
Method:	**Crossbow**	
Classification:	**Irregular**	
Measurements:	**Right**	**Left**
Total Points Side	15	9
Irregular Points Side	10	4
Total Irregular Inches	30	10 1/8
Length of Main Beam	26 6/8	28 1/8
Length of 1st Point	5 2/8	5 6/8
Length of 2nd Point	9 2/8	8 5/8
Length of 3rd Point	12 1/8	11 7/8
Length of 4th Point	5 3/8	9
Length of 5th Point		
Length of 6th Point		
1st Circumference (C1)	5 6/8	5 3/8
2nd Circumference (C2)	5 1/8	4 7/8
3rd Circumference (C3)	4 7/8	5 1/8
4th Circumference (C4)	4 6/8	5 1/8
Score Per Side	109 2/8	94
OFFICIAL SCORE	203 2/8	
Inside Spread	19 3/8	
COMPOSITE SCORE	222 5/8	
Percentage of Irregularity	19.7%	

Mighty Weren't the Preparations
Cody Gwinner Buck

Photo courtesy Cody Gwinner

Taking note of the comings and goings of whitetails on a mere five acres should be as easy as pulling a can of green beans out of the cupboard.

Cody Gwinner and his father, Ted, know their little patch of woods like it was a pantry. And they'd normally have pinpointed the freshest and most often used deer trails long before the season opened, which is where they'd hang or move treestands.

They've also employed trail cameras to get an idea of what kind of deer are moving through their place.

But none of that happened in 2012.

"I normally start glassing the surrounding crop fields in early July and follow through until the season opens and beyond," Cody said. "Last year was different. Between going to work and helping with the family chores, I was just too wrapped up to do any of it.

"Only when the season was upon us did I do a small amount of glassing," he continued. "I probably put in five hours over several days."

Cody saw nothing to excite him during the time he spent with binoculars glued to his eyes. But he did see a couple of very nice 10-pointers cross his own driveway one morning in mid-August. He hoped they'd stick around for a few more weeks.

"Our property is fairly small, but it's mostly wooded, and we're surrounded by acres and acres of food," he said. "Plus, the area has good genetics."

This means that Cody and his dad aren't entirely disadvantaged if they have to head blindly afield, and they've seen or taken numerous deer in the 150-inch range to prove it. Hunting there is a matter of checking the wind and going to whichever stand best accommodates it.

Still, the bucks have to do their part.

When the 2012 archery season opened, Cody was in no hurry to burn a tag. It was hot for October, and the deer weren't anxious to be on their feet until after dark.

He saw only a small 7-pointer during those few early excursions.

"On Nov. 5, my dad and I were on the job, working together. All we talked about was deer hunting, and neither of us expected anything great to happen because we'd not put in the usual time preparing," Cody said.

"I left work at 2:00 that day to pick up my sister at the school bus stop. When we got home, I decided to suit up and spend the rest of the afternoon in a deer stand. I sent a text to my dad, letting him know I was going, and he said he'd join me when he got home from work," he added.

Cody was aloft by 4:00, and Ted climbed into his stand, which was about 80 yards from Cody's, about 4:35. Both men rattled and grunted.

"One of us was making some kind of noise every few minutes," Cody laughed.

At 5:00, Cody saw a small buck approaching from the neighboring property. When he reached for his binoculars, he dropped them. '

"That really made my day," he said.

Fifteen minutes after the unwelcomed thud, Cody heard a crashing noise in front of him and glimpsed a rack in the brush. A buck was following a doe through the high weeds of the nearby CRP field. But they weren't alone.

"There were actually two bucks chasing the doe. And judging from what little I could see, one of them was a shooter," he said. "I immediately grabbed my bow an began digging around for my grunt call, just in case I needed it.

"The doe and the smaller buck were in the lead, and they were going to pass in front of me at about 25 yards," he continued. "Somewhere behind was the other buck. I could hear it grunting and panting in the heat."

Cody drew his bow before he could actually see the deer. He just knew it was closing the gap.

When the rear guard suddenly came into view at 15 yards, Cody bleated softly with his mouth, but the buck ignored him.

"I practically yelled the second time, and that stopped the deer in its tracks," he said. "A split-second later, my arrow smacked it, and the deer actually groaned. Dad even heard it from 80 yards away!

"I knew it was a perfect shot as soon as I

released the arrow," Cody added.

The buck's head went down, and its antlers dragged in the leaves as it tried to gain enough oomph to get out of there. When it did take off, it managed only 40 yards.

Cody couldn't see the downed animal, but he could tell if it moved by watching the weeds.

"I stayed in my stand until dark," he said. "When my dad came over to see what all the commotion had been, I was still sitting there, thinking about the encounter and dealing with about 50 different emotions.

"It had happened so fast, I wasn't sure how big the buck actually was. I didn't have time to get a good look at the antlers or even its body. I just knew from instinct that it was a shooter," he said.

Cody told his father that he'd smoked a big one and that it was lying out in the weeds. While his dad walked in that direction, he began descending his tree.

"I was halfway down when Dad yelled, which made me jump the rest of the way," Cody said.

He considers that moment — standing over the enormous buck with his father — as one of the most exciting moments of his life.

"I would never have taken this deer if it weren't for my father. I owe him a great deal of thanks for all he has done to help me learn about hunting," Cody said.

"From the time I was old enough to accompany

him to the woods, he's taken me along," he added. "He even let me skip high school the first week of November so we could hunt the rut."

After he and Ted had marveled over the bigger-than-expected buck, Cody called and sent text messages and photographs to several of his buddies and to neighbors.

"I was amazed to learn that nobody had ever seen it, that a buck of this caliber had been living in our own back yard, undetected," he said.

"Man, I was just lucky."

Photo courtesy Cody Gwinner

Cody Gwinner Buck

Official Buckmasters Score Sheet		
Taken by:	**Cody Gwinner**	
Date:	**November 5, 2012**	
Location:	**Butler Co., Ohio**	
Method:	**Compound Bow**	
Classification:	**Irregular**	
Measurements:	**Right**	**Left**
Total Points Side	13	14
Irregular Points Side	8	9
Total Irregular Inches	30 5/8	29 4/8
Length of Main Beam	25 1/8	25 6/8
Length of 1st Point	7 5/8	6 6/8
Length of 2nd Point	9 6/8	10 1/8
Length of 3rd Point	11 6/8	9 6/8
Length of 4th Point	8 6/8	7 2/8
Length of 5th Point		
Length of 6th Point		
1st Circumference (C1)	5 7/8	6 3/8
2nd Circumference (C2)	4 7/8	4 6/8
3rd Circumference (C3)	4 3/8	4 4/8
4th Circumference (C4)	5	4 2/8
Score Per Side	113 6/8	109
OFFICIAL SCORE	222 6/8	
Inside Spread	19 6/8	
COMPOSITE SCORE	242 4/8	
Percentage of Irregularity	26.9%	

Hiding in Plain Sight
Bolting buck makes a celebrity of Ohio hunter
Dewey Carpenter Buck

Photo courtesy Dewey Carpenter

On the last Saturday of the 2001 shotgun season, Dewey Carpenter of Gahanna, Ohio, was hunting a farm in Knox County, not far from his home. He was positioned beside a large beech tree at the end of a patch of woods about a half-hour before daylight. Later in the morning, he'd planned on joining his son-in-law, Bobby Ballangee, so that they could make some man-drives.

Within 10 minutes of Dewey's reaching his vantage point, Bobby and Dewey's nephew, Billy, arrived at the farm. In order to get to their stand, the duo had to cross a recently cut cornfield. En route, they jumped a deer from a grassy knoll in the middle of the stubble. They had approached within about 20 yards before it dashed towards the woods.

It was still too dark to see much else, but Bobby could make out the huge rack the deer was wearing. Afterward, he and Billy continued onward.

Nobody saw any deer during the next couple of hours. About 9:00, Bobby and Billy made a small drive toward Dewey's stand, but they jumped no deer. When they joined Dewey, Bobby told his father-in-law about jumping the huge buck in the corn field before dawn. He went on and on about the size of the deer.

The guys then decided to work their way through the woods in the direction the buck had traveled.

They spread out and moved slowly along the windrows toward the far side of the woodlot - hoping to spot the buck. After thoroughly covering the woods, they crossed the corn field and headed back to Bobby's truck.

"We stood by his truck and talked while Bobby

unloaded his gun and prepared to leave," Dewey said. "He had business to attend to.

"I couldn't decide whether to remain in the area or look up a friend and drive to southern Ohio again," he continued. "I finally decided that since I was already there, I might as well stay - at least until noon. This is a good farm to hunt!"

Bobby was ready to leave. He had started his truck while they continued to talk.

"I told him that I was going to go back in and hunt 'til about noon," Dewey said. "So I headed across the cornfield, almost in the same path that Bobby had taken in the darkness that morning. I eventually crossed a fence and wandered into an adjacent field with grass about two feet high. I wanted to walk across that field to make sure nothing was hiding in the tall grass.

"As I walked on into the field, I suddenly saw the huge deer come right up out of the grass about 20 yards in front of me. Because the truck was nearby and still running, and because there was activity about the truck, I was able to approach the buck without his hearing me," Dewey said.

"When the buck stood, it began running at an angle away from me and I was able to get a good clean shot from the side," he continued.

The buck dropped a moment and a few yards later, but it scrambled back up - prompting Dewey to fire a second shot.

As Bobby was closing the gate at the road, he heard the two popping sounds. Figuring that they might have been gunshots, he decided to turn around and drive back toward Dewey, who waved them into the field.

Dewey, Bobby and Billy began tracking the wounded deer across the field, and they saw it get up and try to run.

"The deer was limping severely, but it was still able to move off again, and I got off two more shots," Dewey said. Still, the buck continued into an adjacent field and the trio lost sight of it.

"We spread out and moved ahead. Along the way, I saw what looked like a stump with limbs sticking up in the tall grass. I kept looking at it until I was convinced that it had to be the buck, because the tines were so white. It looked out of place," Dewey said. "I started walking toward it very slowly. When I got closer, it jumped up in front of and facing me. That's when I took my fifth and final shot. The buck dropped right there!"

Afterward, Billy and Bobby came running. The three of them stood in awe of the tremendous buck before field-dressing it and dragging it to the truck. They drove to nearby Johnstown to check the deer in, and a crowd gathered.

"Many people wanted to be photographed with the buck," Dewey said. "I was enjoying the celebrity of it all!"

Photo courtesy Dewey Carpenter

Dewey Carpenter Buck

89

Official Buckmasters Score Sheet		
Taken by:	**Dewey Carpenter**	
Date:	**December 1, 2001**	
Location:	**Knox Co., Ohio**	
Method:	**Shotgun**	
Classification:	**Typical**	
Measurements:	**Right**	**Left**
Total Points Side	9	7
Irregular Points Side	4	3
Total Irregular Inches	4 5/8	5 6/8
Length of Main Beam	30 1/8	28 2/8
Length of 1st Point	7 2/8	7 2/8
Length of 2nd Point	15 4/8	13 3/8
Length of 3rd Point	12 4/8	11
Length of 4th Point	7 7/8	
Length of 5th Point		
Length of 6th Point		
1st Circumference (C1)	5 4/8	5 4/8
2nd Circumference (C2)	4 6/8	4 6/8
3rd Circumference (C3)	5 4/8	5 6/8
4th Circumference (C4)	5 2/8	4 3/8
Score Per Side	98 7/8	86
OFFICIAL SCORE	184 7/8	
Inside Spread	23 1/8	
COMPOSITE SCORE	208	
Percentage of Irregularity	5.5%	

A Buck Barometer Named Chris
With a friend like this, who needs an outfitter
Donnie Wilson Buck

Photo by Don Wilson

It was a slow day at work.

Don Wilson and his partner were sitting in the office when Don's cell phone rang. It was his best huntin' buddy, Chris Snyder, calling to report that the bucks were on the move in Brown County, Ohio. Don looked at his business partner and asked, "You care if I take off early for some hunting?"

Don told Chris he'd be there in two hours. He left for home, loaded up his gear and was on the road inside of 30 minutes, heading south.

"I got there about noon," he said. "Since Chris already had a stand up for me, we just messed around for a while. We headed afield about 2:30.

"It was a quiet evening," Don continued. "All I saw were two does that wandered through just before nightfall. Nothing else was happening, but I sat there 'til well past dark. I lowered most of my gear and headed back to the farmhouse. Chris had already gone to bed. His mother showed me where I would spend the night, and then she made me some dinner. After that, I headed to bed."

Don was back in the same stand well before daylight on Saturday morning, ready for the action Chris had promised.

"It was a bluebird day with just a slight breeze blowing right in my face — perfect for that setup," he said.

About 8:30 or so, he saw a doe off to his left. Behind her was a sizeable buck. They were way too far, walking slowly, so Don tried his grunt call several times. But the deer paid it no mind. Perhaps 100 yards was farther than the sound could carry, or maybe they were too preoccupied to care. Regardless, the pair of whitetails simply walked out of his life.

"It was disappointing. The buck was definitely a shooter, maybe the biggest I'd ever seen," Don remembered. "I thought that was the end of that. I was never going to see them again.

"But about 10 minutes later, I saw another doe — I hoped it was the same one — come out of the trees a short distance from where the two had disappeared earlier. Then I saw a buck come out behind her. It was the same one alright. They were headed slightly in my direction, so I flipped my can call a couple of times.

"The doe started quartering toward me. When she crossed one of the shooting lanes, I ranged her at 45 yards, but she was still moving and quickly closing the distance. When the buck stepped into the lane, I drew my bow, settled my 40-yard pin high on the shoulder and held tight. The doe was headed for a second lane and a tree that I had already ranged at 34 yards. I felt sure that her suitor would follow and present an even better opportunity.

"The buck kept its attention on her, so I stayed at full draw for maybe a minute or two while it moved right past the tree and then stopped. I released the arrow, which sank all the way to the fletching a little low in the chest, stopped by the front leg on the opposite side," Don continued.

"The buck did the high kick thing and ran off. It stopped about 50 yards away and just stood there, looking back toward me, I guess trying to figure out what had happened, what had made the noise or whatever. Then it started to just slowly walk off. It never stumbled or anything; it just walked off.

"After that, I started worrying about the shot. There was nothing I could do, so I decided to stay in the tree for an hour and a half before getting down to look. I looked at my watch: It was 9:00 on the nose. I sat there awhile, and the next time I looked, it was 9:02; the next time, it was 9:05; and the next it was like 10 minutes past. I sat there, waiting for 10:30, probably the longest 90 minutes I ever sat in a stand," Don said.

"By 10:30, I had already packed all my stuff. I got down from the tree and went over to where the deer had been standing. I found good blood, so I followed it to where the deer had stopped to look back. There were two puddles there. I followed the trail for probably another 20 yards and found where the deer had bedded down. I could tell that I'd hit lungs," he added.

Don wanted to get out of the woods and wait awhile longer for the buck to settle down again and die, but he had to exit the same way the deer was traveling. He was careful and watched for blood as he went. He only saw a few more drops before he lost the trail completely. He then headed back to Chris' house, where the two decided to wait until the afternoon before renewing the search.

They returned that evening to the last drops of blood and circled the area for almost three hours until there was no more hope of finding the deer that day. Dejected, Chris and Don returned to the house. All the way, Chris kept telling Don that they would find the buck in the morning; they just needed to keep the faith.

After a very restless night, they resumed searching on Sunday morning. It wasn't long before Chris yelled, "Come over here and see what I just found!"

"He didn't say he found the deer or anything like that. He just said he had something to show me," Don said.

When Don arrived, Chris produced a 6- to 8-inch piece of broken and bloody arrow.

"Well you found my arrow. Did you find any more blood or anything?" Don asked.

"Chris just looked at me and said, quite simply, 'Donny, you just took a 200-inch deer.'

"I said, 'You're kidding me!'"

Chris broke into a smile and got very excited.

"Then Chris took me over to where the deer was lying, and, sure enough, it looked every bit a 200-incher," Don said.

Don stayed with his prize while Chris went back

to the farm to get the deer cart so they could move the deer from the woods to the four-wheeler. At the house, Chris told his dad, Steve, about the buck.

"Calm down, Chris," he replied. "It's probably a big deer, but I doubt it's a 200-incher."

"No, Dad, this is a 200-inch deer. Wait and see!"

Chris returned with the four-wheeler and the deer cart, and they loaded it up and returned to the house. When they got there, Steve looked it over and declared, "Donny boy, you shot a 200-inch deer."

"It was pretty neat how Chris and his dad were both fired up over my taking this deer," Don said. "And I never could have done it without Chris and his well-placed treestand."

Photo by Don Wilson

Donnie Wilson Buck

Official Buckmasters Score Sheet		
Taken by:	Don Wilson	
Date:	November 2, 2007	
Location:	Brown Co., Ohio	
Method:	Compound Bow	
Classification:	Typical	
Measurements:	**Right**	**Left**
Total Points Side	7	7
Irregular Points Side	2	1
Total Irregular Inches	6 3/8	3 1/8
Length of Main Beam	27 4/8	27
Length of 1st Point	8	8 2/8
Length of 2nd Point	12 4/8	12
Length of 3rd Point	12 1/8	12 5/8
Length of 4th Point	8 6/8	8 5/8
Length of 5th Point		1 7/8
Length of 6th Point		
1st Circumference (C1)	4 7/8	5
2nd Circumference (C2)	4 6/8	4 7/8
3rd Circumference (C3)	4 6/8	5 1/8
4th Circumference (C4)	4 4/8	4 7/8
Score Per Side	94 1/8	93 3/8
OFFICIAL SCORE	187 4/8	
Inside Spread	17 1/8	
COMPOSITE SCORE	204 5/8	
Percentage of Irregularity	5.0%	

Rabbits, Ribbing and Other People's Bucks
Eric Williams Buck

Photo courtesy Eric Williams

When Eric Williams and his wife, Angela, grew weary of living in a cramped suburb near Cincinnati, Ohio, they began searching for a place where Eric and their three sons could play outdoors.

In May 2010, they bought a house on 17 acres in Warren County.

You'd think Eric would've spent every spare moment in a deer stand the next fall, but there weren't very many of those.

"With Angela and me both working, and three boys who seem to be into every imaginable sport, I was just strapped for time," he said. "I made a few forays into the back acreage to get a feel for the land. There's a pretty nice patch of woods between two fields, and there was plenty of deer sign."

Eric and his sons erected a double ladder stand in a good spot, but it sat vacant the entire season.

"The next summer, I introduced the boys to a crossbow. I figured they would be able to share it, which would keep costs down," he said. "I also drummed into them the importance of shot placement and maximum range."

When the 2011 season arrived, Eric decided to allow Tanner to hunt alone for the first time, but only if he agreed to stay in the ladder stand, and only when either Eric or Angela were home.

"About two hours into that first hunt, my cell phone rang," he said. "It was Tanner ...

"Well, I hit him," he said. "I found blood!"

"You did what? Come back to the house now," I nearly shouted.

"Tanner returned, we waited for a while, and then we went out and found Tanner's first antlered deer," Eric said. "I couldn't have been prouder ...

and on our OWN piece of land!"

Despite his son's success, Eric was in no hurry to spend time in the stand. It took a friend's taking a beautiful 150-inch buck and an impromptu stroll through his acreage to inspire him.

Chris Mullins, the friend who shot the 150-incher, and another friend, Dave, started ribbing Eric about not hunting. And that led to rabbits.

"We decided for some reason that we would rabbit hunt my property, just to get out there," Eric said. "It was fun, and I saw lots of incredible deer sign. You could smell, see and feel the presence of a dominant buck."

Nov. 28, opening day of gun season, was not ideal for hunting. Eric woke up at 5 a.m., stood on the front porch and listened to the rain.

"Had I hunted the (earlier) rut as hard as I normally do, I wouldn't have considered going out in that stuff," he said. "Now I'm glad I did. It turned out to be one of the best morning hunts I've had in 25 years.

"I saw deer everywhere," he said. "That was the first time anyone had sat in the stand in the morning, and it was amazing, except for the weather. You know how it is: No matter how miserable you are, as long as you're in the woods and seeing deer, it's easy to stay put.

"After seeing about 20 deer, I was pretty excited," he added, "And soaked."

When Eric went home to eat and to get out of his wet clothes, Angela gave him a list of chores. About 2:30, she told him, "I know you want to go hunting, so go!"

"It didn't take much to get me moving in that

direction," Eric said. "After hanging some scent wicks and spraying down with scent-killer, I settled back into the stand at 3:20 p.m. I soon saw my neighbor, Mark, walking along a fencerow about 100 yards distant. I whistled like a bobwhite to get his attention, and he signaled that he was going to walk the property he hunts.

"That morning, I had been grunting and bleating about every half-hour, so I continued that routine in the afternoon. Thirty minutes later, a doe and her yearling sprinted out of the woods, followed by a button buck. The threesome was in a horse pasture that separates our property from the property Mark hunts.

"The button buck wound up 10 yards below my stand, eating honeysuckle, while the doe and yearling faded back into the timber. The wind was at my back, and I'm sure she smelled me, even if she didn't blow and get crazy.

"About 4:30, a massive buck – a shooter – appeared about 125 yards away. I never looked at its rack again. I knew it was bigger than anything I'd ever harvested," he said.

"After I grunted and bleated, it stopped and looked my way, but then it continued following the path the doe had taken.

"Thoughts raced through my head. I was sure the wind was going to keep that buck well away from me. So I got down and began sneaking to get downwind of it, which meant I'd have to cross the field. Fifty yards into it, I changed my mind and went back to the stand.

"Meanwhile, it was pouring down rain," Eric continued.

"As I sat there, drenched and convinced the hunt was finished, I glanced back at the field and saw the buck. It was just standing there at 80 yards, partially obscured by a tree branch. Eventually, the deer started walking toward me, sniffing the air.

"I was worried it would bust me long before I could get off a shot," Eric said. "I was also having a terrible time finding the buck in my fogged-up scope.

"When I finally acquired it, the deer turned broadside and I shot.

"When the smoke cleared, the buck was gone," he added. "Soon afterward, I saw Mark over by the fence, and he didn't appear to have seen anything either.

"I shakily reloaded in the rain, got down from the stand and walked over to Mark. We discussed what had happened, and I told him I thought it was a nice 150-inch 8-pointer.

"Mark hadn't seen anything, so I figured the buck either fell on the spot, or it had run the other way. We decided then to check for sign before it washed away. Close to 30 minutes had passed, and it was getting dark, so we hurried," Eric said.

"When Mark saw my deer, he immediately informed me that it was way more than a 150-incher. While he counted points by the beam of my flashlight, I called the family and Chris.

"Afterward, Mark and I went to the house to get the ATV. By the time we hauled the deer into the garage, quite a crowd had gathered," he said.

The best part?

"A few days later, I took my 11-year-old son, Chase, hunting after work. He was so excited, he was dressed and ready to go before I even pulled off my work shoes. As soon as we settled into the stand, he whispered, 'Dad, can you tell me about how you killed that big buck?'

"Reliving that moment with my son was emotional, something I'll never forget," he said. "I am looking forward to many more days in the woods with Tanner, Chase, Logan and our soon-to-be-born fourth child."

Photo courtesy Eric Williams

Eric Williams Buck

Official Buckmasters Score Sheet		
Taken by:	Eric Williams	
Date:	November 28, 2011	
Location:	Warren Co., Ohio	
Method:	Blackpowder	
Classification:	Irregular	
Measurements:	Right	Left
Total Points Side	11	10
Irregular Points Side	6	5
Total Irregular Inches	15 6/8	17 7/8
Length of Main Beam	24 2/8	23 5/8
Length of 1st Point	6 5/8	6 3/8
Length of 2nd Point	11 1/8	9 5/8
Length of 3rd Point	8 2/8	8 7/8
Length of 4th Point	4	4 3/8
Length of 5th Point		
Length of 6th Point		
1st Circumference (C1)	5 1/8	5 1/8
2nd Circumference (C2)	5	4 7/8
3rd Circumference (C3)	4 5/8	4 6/8
4th Circumference (C4)	3 5/8	3 6/8
Score Per Side	88 3/8	89 2/8
OFFICIAL SCORE	177 5/8	
Inside Spread	17 3/8	
COMPOSITE SCORE	195	
Percentage of Irregularity	18.9%	

Night of the Living Dead
Chris Miraglia Buck

Photo courtesy Chris Miraglia

Chris Miraglia looked like one of George Romero's zombies when he staggered into his suburban Ohio home on Oct. 24, 2011. Had it not been for the goofy grin underneath his bloody and creviced brow his wife might've screamed.

She almost did anyway.

"I got him! I stuck him good!" he mumbled, which, to her, sounded more like "I want to eat your brains!"

And then it registered: Chris had used "him" and "stuck" in the same sentence, which could mean only that he'd put an arrow through Big Boy, a buck with which her husband had become infatuated. But had he field-dressed it with his teeth?

"After I shot Big Boy and saw him lay down, I was hyperventilating," Chris explained. "I was so intent on keeping my eyes on him, I missed the last three steps on the ladder, went down and hit a tree face-first. "I split my forehead wide open and was bleeding pretty profusely," he added. "I was too excited to even care."

Because Chris had literally been hunting in his back yard outside Canton, the last thing he wanted to do was push the buck out of the small copse of woods and onto a neighbor's lawn. So he slept fitfully and didn't return until the following morning.

Chris normally joins his family in southeastern Ohio, where they have a hunting camp. Last fall, however, he opted to stay home and hunt his own little four-acre "wild pocket."

He knew deer inhabited the strip of woods behind his home, but he had no idea a world-class buck was back there until he set out a trail camera his wife gave him for Christmas. When he first pulled the memory card from it on July 21, the die was cast.

"I'd never seen a buck of that caliber in all the years I have been hunting," he said. "And to see it in my own back yard was just tremendous.

"Throughout the summer and into fall, we put out the occasional bit of food right in the yard. Mostly does would take care of that, along with a very nice 8-pointer that we had seen in many photographs with the buck I nicknamed Big Boy," he continued. "About a week before the archery season opened, I put a ladder stand just off the main trail with good shooting lanes in several directions."

Big Boy disappeared after that day, and he stayed gone for six weeks.

"Just that little bit of intrusion into his space was all it took," Chris said.

The big buck's 4x4 buddy continued to visit, however. Chris drew his bow several times during the early season, but he always let off before releasing an arrow. He just couldn't settle for junior, even though he feared someone else had let the air out of Big Boy.

Eventually, desperate times led to desperate

measures.

"I wanted to do whatever I could to get Big Boy back in my territory, I left a drag line of estrous scent through the thicket and to my stand — something I'd read about, but never tried. I did that on Oct. 14, a Friday, in anticipation for my Saturday hunt. That night, my wife and I sat in our kitchen and watched several bucks sparring in the back yard. I got pictures of seven or eight different bucks and several does that weekend, but none of Big Boy or the 8-pointer," he said.

Because the fragrant trail drew in so many bucks, Chris decided to try it again the following Friday. He also hung a scent dripper within range of his stand.

"On Sunday, Oct. 23, I was in the tree when Big Boy suddenly appeared right in front of me. I don't know how he got so close without me seeing him or him seeing me, but there was just no shot before he raised his tail, whirled and disappeared back into the thicket," Chris said. "I knew right away that I was going to be back there the next evening."

Chris was sitting at his computer Monday afternoon, looking at photographs taken from the last memory card he'd pulled from his camera, when the doorbell rang. A good friend, Ed Fox, had come to visit, but Chris didn't have time to chitchat.

"I pretty much told him he couldn't stay, that I had to get ready," he said. "When I showed him a picture of the buck, he knew right away I had buck fever, so he said farewell."

Five minutes after getting dressed, Chris was in his ladder stand. "About 6:45, I heard deer coming. It was the 8-pointer AND Big Boy. When Big Boy came into the open at 55 yards, I went into automatic mode — to the point I don't even remember releasing the arrow, but I sure saw it hit the mark," he said.

"He kicked and fled toward the pond at the back of the thicket," Chris continued. "I saw him lay down after about 67 yards.

"Dark was coming on pretty quickly, so I decided not to disturb him. I didn't want him to bust out of the thicket and into the nearby residential area."

When a sleepy Chris returned at first light on Tuesday, the deer was right where he'd left it. "I dropped to my knees," he said. "Although I'd seen at least 100 trail camera pictures, I still could not believe how big he truly was."

The deer's body was enormous as well.

"I couldn't move him 10 feet, so I went to get my four-wheeler. Even then, I couldn't pull him on the back of it, so I wound up tying him to the back and dragging him to the house," he said. "My brother showed up just as I got there, and he helped me hang it."

Photo courtesy Chris Miraglia

Chris Miraglia Buck

Official Buckmasters Score Sheet		
Taken by:	Christopher Miraglia	
Date:	October 24, 2011	
Location:	Stark Co., Ohio	
Method:	Compound Bow	
Classification:	Semi-Irregular	
Measurements:	Right	Left
Total Points Side	11	7
Irregular Points Side	6	2
Total Irregular Inches	14 3/8	3 3/8
Length of Main Beam	24 3/8	24 4/8
Length of 1st Point	10	9 7/8
Length of 2nd Point	9 4/8	9
Length of 3rd Point	10 7/8	8 6/8
Length of 4th Point	7	5 6/8
Length of 5th Point		
Length of 6th Point		
1st Circumference (C1)	5 3/8	5 2/8
2nd Circumference (C2)	5 1/8	4 5/8
3rd Circumference (C3)	5 3/8	5 4/8
4th Circumference (C4)	4 5/8	4 4/8
Score Per Side	96 5/8	81 1/8
OFFICIAL SCORE	177 6/8	
Inside Spread	24 5/8	
COMPOSITE SCORE	202 3/8	
Percentage of Irregularity	9.9%	

Grandpa Mac Was Right
Tall tale turns out to be not so tall after all.
Peter Johnston Buck

Photo courtesy Peter Johnston

Peter Johnston's family has maintained a camp in Burnett County, Wis., west of Shell Lake, for three generations. His grandfather, Mac Johnston, found the place many moons ago.

The original building was a 1940s-era blacksmith shop. The Johnstons eventually built a small cabin next door for sleeping, but the old shop is where they forge bonds over cards and tall tales.

Most of the hunting land there is broken into 40- to 80-acre blocks, separated by cropland and pastures. Since there are no large farms or unbroken forest, they always hunt with the locals they've befriended over many years.

By joining with the local farmers, much more land is accessible, and this allows them to stage man-drives of large sections of timbered land.

"Our group customarily hunts from stands for the first few hours of the day. Then, after the local farmers finish their chores, they join us for man-drives of each section," Peter said.

"My family lives about 60 miles away from this area, and many of us are able to hunt only a week at the start of gun season. My dad, Pete, and Uncle Jeff were also in camp last year.

"The first day of the season was very slow for me. I saw only a few deer. The second morning, Nov. 22, we hunted from our stands until midmorning, and then we began to organize the drives. Fifteen of us were there.

"We decided to first hit a nearby 40 that we'd driven the previous day, even though we hadn't seen anything run out of there. It was my turn to be a stander, and I took a position just inside the woods," the 26-year-old continued. "I found a good

115

sized stump and stood on it for a better view. The woods were pretty open; I could see about 200 yards in some directions.

"I had just glanced at my watch and noted that it was only 9:30, earlier than usual to be making drives, when I saw antlers about 200 yards from me. A buck was coming toward me at a steady clip, but not running.

"I shouldered my rifle and prepared to take the shot, not really knowing how big a rack it carried. I waited until it was in a safe shooting lane so I couldn't possibly hit any of the drivers, and then I took what amounted to a 60-yard shot.

"The buck never flinched, so I immediately shot again. That time, it ran out onto the road skirting the woods, stopped right in the middle, and then turned to look back at me. That buck looked more like an elk than a deer. It carried a very large and wide set of antlers.

"After crossing the road, it dropped down into a swamp and kept right on running, as far as I could tell," he said.

Once the buck left the road, Peter could no longer see the animal or which way it headed after entering the swamp. Nothing else came from the woods. Soon, all the drivers gathered around Peter to hear what had happened.

The group walked to where Peter thought he'd last seen the giant and began looking for signs of a hit. No one could find even a single drop of blood, but they continued to search.

Suddenly, a first-year hunter named Alecia sang out that she had found a large splatter of blood near the roadside. The group joined her, saw the red stuff and looked down into the swamp, where they saw antlers rising above the undergrowth. The buck had traveled only 30 yards after crossing the road.

"Up until that moment, I wasn't sure I'd even hit the deer," Peter said. "I don't think I was shaking, but I'm not an expert shot either. When I shoot at a deer, I either get the shakes, or I'm perfectly calm. If I have the shakes, I usually connect with the target; when I'm calm, I usually miss.

"Immediately after the shot, I started shaking, but they subsided when I thought I'd missed the buck. I sure didn't see any reaction from the deer to indicate a good hit, so I was very happy to see it lying there," Peter said. "When I laid eyes on those antlers, I started shaking so badly that I had to ask another hunter, Mike, to do the field-dressing so I wouldn't stab myself."

When the hunter stepped out of the check station, a crowd of about 30 people had gathered to look at his deer. Everyone was amazed at the antlers. Nobody had seen or heard of such a buck in the area, except for maybe Peter's grandfather the previous season.

"Grandpa Mac had developed cancer before the 2008 season. As a result, even though he went hunting with us that year, he was only able to sit in the old shack that used to be the camp.

"There was a story about him seeing a "monster buck" during his time at the shack. But Mac was known to be a teller of tall tales, and every buck he saw was a true monster. So it was likely I was never told because the others at camp just assumed it was probably another embellishment," Peter said.

"Big bucks are not common in this part of Wisconsin because deer cause a lot of crop damage. Pretty much any buck or doe is taken if they present a shot to a hunter," he added.

Mac Johnston died between the 2008 and 2009 seasons. But Peter thinks the old man might have been there in spirit to bring hunter and hunted together.

Peter has since talked to other farmers in the area who told him several people spent the entire year hunting for that particular buck.

"Someone said a fellow from a town downstate tagged it. I was a bit unsure if I should tell them that I was the guy. I guess if they read this, they'll finally know the truth," Peter said.

Photo courtesy Peter Johnston

Peter Johnston Buck

119

Official Buckmasters Score Sheet		
Taken by:	**Peter Johnston**	
Date:	**November 22, 2009**	
Location:	**Burnett Co., WI**	
Method:	**Modern Rifle**	
Classification:	**Irregular**	
Measurements:	**Right**	**Left**
Total Points Side	7	6
Irregular Points Side	3	2
Total Irregular Inches	18 7/8	13 6/8
Length of Main Beam	28 2/8	28
Length of 1st Point	5 3/8	5
Length of 2nd Point	15 6/8	14 2/8
Length of 3rd Point	12 1/8	8 7/8
Length of 4th Point		
Length of 5th Point		
Length of 6th Point		
1st Circumference (C1)	5 4/8	5 1/8
2nd Circumference (C2)	5	4 7/8
3rd Circumference (C3)	5 5/8	5 3/8
4th Circumference (C4)	6 4/8	5 2/8
Score Per Side	103	90 4/8
OFFICIAL SCORE	193 4/8	
Inside Spread	23 7/8	
COMPOSITE SCORE	217 3/8	
Percentage of Irregularity	16.8%	

Rip Van Winkle Shoots Modern Day Legend
Brian Peters Buck

Photo courtesy Brian Peters

Brian Peters Buck

Thirty-six-year-old Brian Peters drives a dump truck for a living, hauling asphalt out of a plant in Byesville, Ohio. During the summer, he works long hours, usually seven-day weeks.

There is little time for anything but work until the weather turns cold and most highway paving stops, and then he gets behind the wheel of a tractor-trailer and hauls coal, stone and slag. Still, Brian is thankful for the shorter days and less work in the fall, before the furnaces' bellies start grumbling.

Even with the sputtering economy, there was still plenty of highway resurfacing work to keep him hauling in late 2009. But Brian wasn't so busy that he couldn't devote an hour or two in the evenings to sitting in a box stand on his sixteen and a half acres near Caldwell, Ohio.

He had more than his usual love of deer hunting to inspire him last season. He'd seen several nice bucks on his and the adjacent coal company's lands, including a deer with a nickname.

"Tall Boy had been seen throughout the neighborhood for three years," Brian said. "He was a very long-tined 10-pointer. One neighbor even took a picture of him inside his fenced garden plot, in broad daylight."

Brian lusted after that deer. He decided to settle for nothing less, except maybe a doe for the freezer.

He wasn't able to hunt Monday, Nov. 15, but he was inside his box stand every evening thereafter. He saw a forkhorn on Tuesday, on Wednesday, a decent 6-pointer, and an 8-pointer on Thursday. All the bucks were interested in does. The 4x4, Brian knew, had traveled with Tall Boy earlier in the year.

The small-to-large progression of bucks from Tuesday through Thursday put an extra spring in Brian's step as he headed to his vantage point on Friday. He even got off work earlier than usual.

"I got home by 2:30, but I was exhausted," he said. "I almost took a nap, but I showered and made a peanut butter-and-jelly sandwich.

"It was probably 3:30 when I climbed the ladder and settled in for the evening," he continued. "It was very warm. I remember eating the sandwich, but little else because I soon fell asleep. Several times I nearly fell off the stool, but then, jarred awake, I'd sit up straight and look around some more.

"At some point, I heard noises and realized deer were close. Some does were coming into the clearing to feed, as usual, and I dozed off again," he said.

When more rustling woke Brian, he glanced up and saw a big buck jump the neighbor's fence and head into a thick stand of trees about 15 yards beyond and slightly downhill from the feeding does.

"I didn't get a good look at it," he said. "I just knew it was a shooter buck, for sure. It raised its head and curled its lip, obviously checking to see if any of the does were hot. About all I could see at that point was the front of its head, some of the antlers and its backside.

"I had already made the decision to take any shot it presented, so I shouldered my crossbow," Brian continued. "The buck eventually turned back toward the fence. As soon as I had a clear lane at about 32 yards, I squeezed the trigger."

The deer bucked in response, and then it fled.

"It ran off pretty quickly, making lots of noise, and was soon out of sight ... but still making lots of noise," Brian said. "And then, suddenly, everything was quiet. I never heard a crash."

Brian knew he should give the buck some time, even though he'd never shot one with a crossbow. At least that's what he'd heard and read. He also wanted to put his hands on it before dark, which was fast approaching.

Good sense won out, though, and he went home to stew in his own juices.

"I called my good friend and neighbor, Duane, to see if he and his wife could come over to help me track the deer," Brian said. "While I was waiting for them, I decided to feed my horses and get that chore done for the evening as I expected there was a long night ahead.

"When my neighbors arrived, we headed back into my woods to take up the trail. From the box stand, I went straight to the point of impact. We searched by flashlight for blood and my arrow, and we found both. The bolt was covered in blood, and there was a pretty good trail.

"I measured the distance back to the stand at 32 yards, about what I'd figured before I made the shot. We took up the trail and easily followed drops and splashes right up to the buck. For the record and my own curiosity, I later stepped it off at 83 yards from impact to where the deer fell.

"As soon as our flashlight beams illuminated the rack, there was no doubt that I'd shot Tall Boy. I fell to my knees and lifted the head to count and recount the points."

At a casual glance, the buck is a 10-pointer -- a

clean and very impressive 5x5. But each antler also has a sixth scoreable point at the burr. The extra 2 3/8 inches of irregularity nudge the rack into the typical category, where it's No. 7 among crossbow-taken entries.

"I was awestruck," Brian said.

"My neighbor took cell phone photos and sent them to just about everyone on his contacts list as well to some of my friends. Afterward, we started dragging," he added.

By the time they arrived at Brian's house, less than 700 yards from where they started, several cars were already parked in the driveway. Many more gawkers followed, even as late as 11 p.m.

"After everybody left, we took Tall Boy down to hang in my neighbor's garage. More people dropped by to see it there, too," Brian said. "I don't know how late it was when I finally got home, but even though I had been tired all day, I had trouble falling asleep."

Photo Courtesy Ed Waite

Brian Peters Buck

Official Buckmasters Score Sheet		
Taken by:	**Brian Peters**	
Date:	**November 20, 2009**	
Location:	**Noble Co., Ohio**	
Method:	**Crossbow**	
Classification:	**Typical**	
Measurements:	**Right**	**Left**
Total Points Side	6	6
Irregular Points Side	1	1
Total Irregular Inches	1 1/8	1 2/8
Length of Main Beam	28 4/8	28 2/8
Length of 1st Point	3 7/8	3 6/8
Length of 2nd Point	11 1/8	13 7/8
Length of 3rd Point	14 2/8	13 6/8
Length of 4th Point	9 7/8	9 4/8
Length of 5th Point		
Length of 6th Point		
1st Circumference (C1)	4 2/8	4 3/8
2nd Circumference (C2)	4 1/8	4 2/8
3rd Circumference (C3)	4 5/8	4 5/8
4th Circumference (C4)	4 7/8	4 5/8
Score Per Side	86 5/8	88 2/8
OFFICIAL SCORE	174 7/8	
Inside Spread	19 2/8	
COMPOSITE SCORE	194 1/8	
Percentage of Irregularity	1.3%	

From the Land of SHE-DEER
Unlike the monsters under beds and in closets, this Ohio buck is the real deal.
Brett McGuire Buck

Photo courtesy of Ed Waite

When the McGuires go hunting, it's more like grocery shopping.

Ohio might be home to the country's most prosperous taxidermists, and Mahoning might be one of the few counties even nonresident hunters are able to cite. But the public and neighboring ground this family has prowled for the last decade has been little more than the Land of Does and Little-Bitty bucks.

Until last year. "My father Jim, brothers Jimmy and Darin and I have hunted a large section of public land in northeastern Ohio for many years," said Brett McGuire. "We never know who might also be hunting beyond the next rise."

The inherent danger of sharing the woods with all comers is what eventually spurred the family's menfolk to ask for permission to hunt a neighboring tract.

"We'd noticed that just across the road from where we hunt was a farm with lots of timber, and it didn't look like anyone was hunting it," Brett said. "I approached the landowner, Jim Gatto, one day, and he granted us permission to hunt his 40 acres."

That was 10 years ago, and the McGuires have hunted that piece of property ever since.

"There's a very good deer population on that farm," Brett said, "and it draws a lot of animals from the public land when the pressure gets heavy."

"Throughout all those years, however, we mostly harvested does. We just don't see many mature bucks," he added.

Not that the men complained, though, since does make better venison.

"Nevertheless, we try to hunt religiously," Brett said. "Every day of archery or gun season, if we can, we're out there somewhere."

"One day in 2012, when things were really slow, I lowered myself from my tree and decided to do some still-hunting, thinking I might come across a better setup," he continued. "I was crossing back and forth from public to private land when I came to an area that showed a lot of promise."

"There were several scrapes, droppings and a couple of torn-up trees," he said.

"I retrieved my climber and returned to set up on a low ridge overlooking this hot spot. I was just off the private land by a few hundred feet."

"Just after 1:00, I heard splashing in the creek behind me. It was like a plunking sound as each foot splashed in the stream," Brett continued. "I quickly spun around in my stand and looked, but I didn't see anything.

"I knew something was coming. I heard it when it jumped up on the bank, and I could even see mud swirling in the water where the deer had crossed, but I couldn't see anything that even remotely looked like a deer."

And then he did.

When the buck stepped out from behind a huge oak tree, Brett could see only its right antler. The mass was incredible. He'd never seen such in the wild.

"The deer was at 20 yards when I drew my bow, but there was no shot, at first," he said. "It was angling away from me. I knew it was about to walk out of my life forever, so I decided to take a less – than – ideal shot.

"When the buck finally stopped at 40 yards and lowered its head, I squeezed my release's trigger. The arrow entered just behind the rib cage — a bit far back, but I thought it wasn't bad for the angle."

"When the deer bolted, I could see the arrow protruding from its left side," he added.

Afterward, Brett quickly sent a text message to his brother, Jimmy, who was sitting several hundred yards away.

"You're full of it," Jimmy answered. "There are no monsters around here!"

"No, I'm dead serious," Brett replied.

"Was it a good hit?"

'I think I hit pretty far back. Might be a gut shot."

Half an hour later, Jimmy texted again: "Are you down out of the tree yet?"

"No, I'm giving it some time."

"Well, how much time are you going to give it?"

Brett had already started descending.

"When I got over there, I found hair, blood and even some pieces of flesh, so I felt considerably better about the whole thing," he said. "Jimmy and I bantered back and forth as he questioned me, until he was almost convinced I might be telling the truth."

"Alright, I'm getting down. I'll be over in a few minutes," Jimmy typed.

The brothers took up the blood trail I5 minutes later, but the tap shutoff when the buck went uphill. Brett thought he'd seen it heading for the field up top, but the deer actually veered when it was out of sight, jumping over a drainage ditch before going deeper into the woods.

"Jimmy then remembered that he'd heard a crash near his stand, and we began a somewhat methodical search in that direction. We pushed through some of the thickest brush on the property, but to no avail," Brett said.

"After an hour, I was really disgusted with myself and threw my bow down, declaring that if I had only wounded the deer, I was done with hunting. I was that disgusted!"

Jimmy, trying to soothe his brother's angst, pointed out that there was still plenty of time to hunt, a declaration that the deer was lost, without saying as much.

"I am going back and starting all over again," Brett told him.

Jimmy went with him. That time when they ran out of blood near the ditch, they made a wider circle and Brett found two puddles where the buck had bedded. Brett was looking at the blood when Jimmy said, "There it is!"

"By the time I turned to look, the buck was on its feet," Brett said. "It made two bounds, and then went back to ground."

Rather than push the wounded buck, the brothers went back to their truck to wait, where they were soon joined by their father, the landowner and his son. For the next hour, Brett was peppered with questions.

When they returned to look for the deer, Jimmy circled around front, hoping the buck, if still alive, might run back toward Brett, who had another arrow nocked and ready. Jimmy saw it first, and when he was 20 yards away, the animal stood and ran another 60 yards, but not toward Brett.

"That's it!" Brett said. "Let's back out of here and wait until tomorrow."

When they returned the next morning, they found the buck curled around a tree, its head upright, which gave them pause, but only because the antlers had caught the tree and were supporting the dead deer's head.

"I walked in slowly," Brett said. "When I got in real close, I kicked it in the butt, it didn't move."

The guys took several photographs of the deer where they found it, but except for the ones they snapped with Brett's cell phone, all were lost.

"It's funny," Brett smiled. "My dog chewed up the memory card. Really!"

133

Photo courtesy of Ed Waite

Brett McGuire Buck

Official Buckmasters Score Sheet		
Taken by:	**Brett McGuire**	
Date:	**November 10, 2012**	
Location:	**Mahoning Co., Ohio**	
Method:	**Compound Bow**	
Classification:	**Irregular**	
Measurements:	**Right**	**Left**
Total Points Side	10	11
Irregular Points Side	6	7
Total Irregular Inches	12 1/8	21
Length of Main Beam	26 3/8	26 7/8
Length of 1st Point	8 6/8	8 6/8
Length of 2nd Point	11 2/8	12
Length of 3rd Point	8	7 6/8
Length of 4th Point		
Length of 5th Point		
Length of 6th Point		
1st Circumference (C1)	5 7/8	5 3/8
2nd Circumference (C2)	4 3/8	4 5/8
3rd Circumference (C3)	4 3/8	4 3/8
4th Circumference (C4)	4 1/8	3 4/8
Score Per Side	85 2/8	94 2/8
OFFICIAL SCORE	179 4/8	
Inside Spread	19 1/8	
COMPOSITE SCORE	198 5/8	
Percentage of Irregularity	19.4%	

Parting Gift
Hunting property yields bittersweet trophy
Gene Figge Buck

Photo courtesy Gene Figge

Gene Figge had no way of knowing that the 2004 season would be his last to hunt the Jersey County, Ill., farm his family had enjoyed for nearly three decades. About a month after deer season ended, the landowner died, and the property was sold.

The new owners have not been as generous.

But while the '04 season ended on a sour note for the Figges, it began with a bang.

Literally.

Opening day of shotgun season found Gene hunting the farm with his father, Dennis. Even the worst weather couldn't keep them indoors, since the season lasted only three days.

"I was up in a climber stand," Gene said. "The weather was bad and getting worse. It was in the mid - 30s and raining. The wind ate through my clothes and chilled me to the bone. I saw one small buck about 9:30, but it was too far away to even try a shot. Not long afterward, I was ready to quit."

Gene had already envisioned where he was going to move his stand for the evening hunt. While packing his gear in preparation for returning to the truck, a shot rang out from where Dennis was hunting. So instead of heading for the vehicle, Gene trotted off toward his dad's stand.

When he arrived a few minutes later, Dennis told him he'd shot a doe. And while father and son were planning where to drag her, Dennis noticed several very fresh rubs along a trail.

"I decided to hang my stand right there," Gene said. "I picked a tree, left my stand and some gear, and then we dragged Dad's doe toward the truck."

After lunch and a change into dry clothes, Gene returned to the woods for the afternoon in a much better mood. The weather had improved, too.

"I got situated in the stand around 2:30, warmer and certainly dryer than I had been that morning," he said. "I didn't see anything, not even a squirrel, until the last hour. With 45 minutes of daylight remaining, a deer blew. I could hear brush snapping just over the ridge top. It sounded like the deer was racing along the other side of the ridge.

And then, suddenly, a doe popped over the crest between 30 and 35 yards away.

"She was the one snorting, and a nice 10-pointer was a few steps behind her," he added.

"The two deer were moving pretty fast and headed right for me. I tried to get ready for a shot, but they never slowed. I grunted with my mouth several times, and then I resorted to yelling at them. But they kept on moving, passing almost directly under my stand. I hollered 'Stop' and maybe a few other choice words, but they kept on truckin'."

As soon as the deer disappeared, Gene sat down and tried to regain his wits.

His breath was ragged, and he was starting to shake as the adrenaline flowed through his body.

"Man, that was a nice buck, and I never had a shot," he said. "I could not believe how quickly it had all happened. The whole scenario played out in maybe two or three minutes, total.

"A second later, however, I heard more brush cracking," he continued. "It was coming from the exact area where the other two had appeared. I zeroed-in on the same spot where the doe had crossed over and got ready. I saw antler tips, and then they grew taller and taller. I thought I'd never see the head to which they were attached.

"When the buck finally broke over the top of the ridge, it was on the same path the others had taken. I knew it would follow the same trail. I also knew that, at the speed it was moving, I wouldn't get a clean shot at it either.

"This guy was grunting with every step, way too fast. It was past me in a few seconds. I swung around in the stand as the buck headed up the big ridge. I led it a few feet and pulled the trigger," Gene said. "I didn't think I'd hit it, but it stopped for just the few seconds I needed to jack in another shell, aim and pull the trigger. The buck bolted, changed direction and was out of sight within seconds.

"I could hear it moving away, making a lot of noise as it plowed through the brush. Those sounds were followed by a very loud crash, and then I could've sworn I heard something sliding down the side of the hill. After that, everything was silent."

Gene's mind was reeling. He wanted to believe he'd just heard the buck go to ground. But he was not sure. He hurriedly unloaded his gun and came down the tree in the fading light.

"I didn't want to lose the chance to get on the track before dark. Maybe the last sounds I heard were of the buck getting out of range, maybe not. I actually closed my eyes and walked right to spot where the buck had stopped after I made the first shot. There on the ground was a spray of crimson. I had connected after all!

"I walked a more few feet as I tried to see in my mind where I had aimed for the second shot. I was fairly sure I had been on the rib cage when I pulled, but I was pretty excited.

"About three steps farther on, I found more blood and even a piece of rib bone. That did it for me. I was sure it was down somewhere.

"I hollered for my dad and told him I had hit a really big buck, and he came running. I told him how big it was, but I don't think he believed me," he continued. "We started following the trail. Dad was looking at the blood, while I was scanning the woods for either a white belly or antlers. I saw the deer first."

It had traveled a mere 50 yards.

Dennis took one quick look, and then said, "That's not a big deer that's a GREAT BIG DEER."

"We had never seen anything like it in all our years of hunting," Gene said.

After admiring the buck and exchanging high-fives, they decided to drag the animal to the bottom — which they hoped to reach by ATV — rather than up the ridge. They were at the check station with the buck a couple of hours later, where the attendant aged it at 7 1/2 years old.

While caping the deer, Gene's taxidermist found a 2-inch-long antler tip, broken off and embedded in the deer's skull in front of the eye socket. The eye was intact and appeared to have been functioning, but the area was infected.

Photo courtesy Ed Waite

Gene Figge Buck

Official Buckmasters Score Sheet		
Taken by:	**Robert 'Gene' Figge**	
Date:	**November 19, 2004**	
Location:	**Jersey Co., Illinois**	
Method:	**Shotgun**	
Classification:	**Irregular**	
Measurements:	**Right**	Left
Total Points Side	8	10
Irregular Points Side	3	5
Total Irregular Inches	8 4/8	17 2/8
Length of Main Beam	25 5/8	21 5/8
Length of 1st Point	8 4/8	6 7/8
Length of 2nd Point	11 6/8	10 7/8
Length of 3rd Point	12 2/8	12 2/8
Length of 4th Point	3 7/8	5 1/8
Length of 5th Point		
Length of 6th Point		
1st Circumference (C1)	5 7/8	6 1/8
2nd Circumference (C2)	4 2/8	4 4/8
3rd Circumference (C3)	4	3 7/8
4th Circumference (C4)	3 6/8	3 5/8
Score Per Side	88 3/8	92 1/8
OFFICIAL SCORE	180 4/8	
Inside Spread	18 5/8	
COMPOSITE SCORE	199 1/8	
Percentage of Irregularity	14.2%	

Why Leonard was Late for Church
Hunters on both sides of the Red River were gunning for this driftwood-wearing buck
Andy Anderson Buck

Photo courtesy of Andy Anderson

This story is not about Leonard Ernst, but it might explain why he almost skipped Sunday morning services last Nov. 7.

It most definitely accounts for the bare pew in Andy Anderson's church.

Andy didn't intend to play hooky that day, but he had his hands full with a deer he shot during an impromptu, pre-church hunt.

He hadn't been able to spend much time in the woods last year, not since the fire exactly one month earlier. So when he saw an opportunity, even a tiny little window, he seized it.

Andy hunts a mostly open 600-acre lease in Louisiana's Red River Parish. It's not exactly teeming with whitetails, he says, but the tract is a funnel for deer movement between places with more cover.

On Oct. 7, the man from Coushatta, La., lost his enthusiasm, as well as his means, for hunting. That's when his home pretty much burned to the ground, the blaze hotter than even his high-dollar gun safe could withstand.

"It was a terrible shock to see everything we owned gone," Andy said. "The only thing salvaged was my father's Model 12 shotgun, though the fore-end was burnt. The inspector said the fire must have reached at least 2,000 degrees for all the damage that was done."

Andy and his wife moved into a travel trailer in the back yard while their house was being rebuilt.

"Hunting season was on the back burner as we worked on getting things back to normal," he said. "Buying a gun was the last thing on my mind."

A couple of weeks after the fire, a cousin loaned

Andy a .270 and a shotgun. The rifle had an old 4x scope that had seen better days, but it was warmly received.

"I made a few trips to check my stands when I had time," Andy said. "I hunted a little, too.

"I had intended to hunt Saturday evening, Nov. 6, but I was called in to work. It was after midnight when I got off and headed home. Needless to say, I slept in Sunday morning.

"When I did get moving, I decided to watch the LSU highlights and check my e-mails. Afterward, I told the wife I was going to go out and sit for a bit before church," he continued.

Andy arrived at his lease about 7:30 and struck out for his "middle stand," which seemed best for the wind. Upon nearing it, he crested a high spot and saw a buck with a nice rack about 150 yards away in a bottom.

"I ran the last 50 feet to my stand because I needed a steady rest for such a long shot," he said. "I propped on one of the cross members, and, when I finally found the buck in the scope, squeezed the trigger."

The deer dropped like a bag of rocks, though Andy would take a second shot to anchor it.

"I think that old scope might deserve a lot of credit," he said. "Had it been a newer or more powerful model, I might have had a clearer picture of what I was shooting at, and I might've blown that first shot.

"All I really knew was that the deer had a rack," he added.

After administering the coup de grace, Andy paused to give thanks and to admire the gnarly antlers, which looked strangely familiar.

It had to be the same buck he'd shot at in 2008. The deer stopped broadside in the center of a pipeline at last light, but Andy didn't cut a hair.

Nobody had seen the buck since that day. Andy had even convinced himself that the tangle of antlers he'd seen must have been an 8-pointer with vegetation entangled in its rack.

Now he knew better.

After examining the freakish antlers, Andy called his hunting buddy, Leonard Ernst, to ask for help. Leonard and his wife were getting ready for church, but Andy convinced him to make the short drive.

"I told him the gate was open, and to just drive straight back to the stand. We could load it on his truck, and then run it out to mine," Andy said. "When he got there, we shared some serious excitement before doing the truck shuffle. I practically had to force Leonard to get back home and go to church before his wife got mad at both of us.

"I stopped at his house to weigh the deer, which went 230 pounds," Andy continued, "and then I took it to my cousin's so his wife could take pictures and send them to her husband, who was hunting in Illinois. They live right next door, so I was essentially hunting in our back yards.

"By the time I hung the deer at my house, a steady stream of people began arriving to take a look at the unusual rack," he said. "We counted those points many times."

Andy's taxidermist, Wayne Gates, said the deer was at least 8 1/2 years old. It was almost toothless.

"I learned later that a hunter across the Red River had trail camera photographs of this buck eating oat bran from his feeder at midnight Saturday, one and a half miles north of where I took it Sunday morning," Andy said. "This guy got around."

Photo courtesy of Andy Anderson

Andy Anderson Buck

Official Buckmasters Score Sheet		
Taken by:	**Andy Anderson**	
Date:	**November 7, 2010**	
Location:	**Red River Parish, Louisiana**	
Method:	**Modern Rifle**	
Classification:	**Irregular**	
Measurements:	**Right**	Left
Total Points Side	13	12
Irregular Points Side	9	9
Total Irregular Inches	56	45 3/8
Length of Main Beam	19 4/8	19
Length of 1st Point	5 3/8	6
Length of 2nd Point	6 2/8	12 2/8
Length of 3rd Point		
Length of 4th Point		
Length of 5th Point		
Length of 6th Point		
1st Circumference (C1)	5	4 6/8
2nd Circumference (C2)	4 4/8	4 2/8
3rd Circumference (C3)	9 5/8	4 7/8
4th Circumference (C4)	2 3/8	2 3/8
Score Per Side	108 5/8	98 7/8
OFFICIAL SCORE	207 4/8	
Inside Spread	14 6/8	
COMPOSITE SCORE	222 2/8	
Percentage of Irregularity	48.8%	

Oh Buck, Where Art thou
When the eyes of men and the nose of dogs fail
Steve Esker Buck

Photo courtesy Steve Esker

If the name Esker sounds familiar and the photo on the cover looks even more so, you might want to look back at the Winter 2009 issue of Rack magazine. The smiling hunter is Scott Esker, shown with his 2008 buck. This time, Steve Esker's out front with his '09 bruiser.

They're twin brothers, both avid deer hunters in Ohio. The Eskers are gaga over whitetails, and they're in the woods throughout the year, scouting if not hunting.

Trail cameras are in place and working all year 'round, keeping track of the old boys and the up-and-comers.

Prior to the 2008 season, Scott and Steve acquired a parcel they'd hunted for eight years. They knew the land very well and immediately set about planting food plots and erecting stands for various winds.

Steve had picked out two bucks that year. He passed on several 150-inchers while holding out for one of the big boys. He figured the largest would top 180 inches.

Scott tied his tag to a monster that year while hunting a different tract. Steve wound up eating his tag. But at least nobody else shot the deer he was hoping to see in his sights.

The waiting game began anew in September 2009. Steve passed on a nice 150-inch buck his very first night in a stand. Knowing there were four months of archery season ahead of him, he was in no hurry to settle for a lesser deer. He was convinced it was just a matter of time before the bull of the woods showed.

On the season's fourth overcast evening, the

wind was perfect for that same spot. Deer were feeding all around the setup that day. A few does and smaller bucks were first, followed by a familiar 10-pointer. Steve was pumped.

"I had my video camera attached to the tree and was able to look at the display while seated. I had already shot some footage of deer passing my stand," he said. "The does were feeding off to the east of me when, suddenly, something spooked them.

"There was a lot of blowing and stomping, and then they all ran back toward me. However, the excitement was short lived; everybody calmed down and eventually started feeding again," he added.

"Twenty-five minutes later, I looked up the fencerow and saw THE buck. There was no mistaking that fellow, standing in the clover patch right in front of my other stand, about 130 yards away. It was browsing and scoping out the other deer in the field.

"The buck was moving toward me, so I turned on the video camera, pointed it in the right direction, and then I stood slowly so I could more easily turn to face the buck as it approached. My crossbow was ready," he continued.

"The deer moved right-to-left and into the food plot just in front of me. I was almost frantically trying to move the video camera with my right leg as the deer passed in front of me," Steve added. "I managed to keep the deer in the screen, but I don't know how.

"That buck must have had a sixth sense. Every time it moved, it ended up behind some obstruction that blocked my shot. After what seemed like hours, it approached an opening where I could thread the needle.

"By then, the adrenaline was pumping and my heart was pounding so loud I was surprised the deer didn't hear it. At 20 yards, it stepped into the clear and I squeezed the trigger. I watched the arrow fly to the target. It was a good shot; the bolt passed right through, and the deer disappeared.

"I'd been concentrating so hard I didn't notice that several other deer had moved into the foot plot, including three other bucks. At the sound of the shot, every deer in the field bolted toward the tall grass and trees beyond.

"Deer were running everywhere, helter-skelter, and I lost my buck in the group," he continued. "I sat down to catch my breath and regain my senses, and then I took the video camera in hand to review what happened.

"The footage showed the arrow entered just a little below where I had aimed, but it was a pretty good hit. But that's all I could tell. When the deer bolted, it was almost instantly out of the camera's view," he said.

Steve called his brother, and they decided to go to the house for a while and to look at the video on the television screen to help determine where the buck ran. But it didn't help.

The guys then returned to the farm and started the search, but it had started to rain by then, which didn't help matters. All of their searching produced a single spot of blood, and there was no hope of following the trail in the dark.

The next day, Steve contacted a man who has a

tracking dog. After a good bit of searching and sniffing, the dog never picked up the trail. They realized later they'd put the dog in the wrong place, where there was no trail to follow.

By midday, the searchers were frustrated and stopped for lunch. Steve recruited a few more sets of eyes, and they returned to find a buzzard flying overheard. They concentrated below it, but after all that was searched, there was still no deer.

Finally, the remaining hunters wanted to be in their stands for the evening hunt, so that left Scott and Steve to go it alone.

Steve's frustration was nearing the boiling point. He knew the monster was out there somewhere. He also knew that he would do whatever it took to recover the deer.

Back at home, he fired up his computer and started looking for where he could rent a helicopter. He found Fairfield Air Adventures and pilot Steve Slater, who was game to come out and help.

"I described the exact location of the farm and the field and a nearby place where he could land to pick me up. He knew the area and told me he would be there very soon and that I should meet him there.

"Slater landed at about 5 p.m., and we were back in the air within minutes. As soon as the helicopter was in the air above the field, I saw the deer lying in the 6-foot-tall grass. The pilot landed, and I got out and ran over to it.

"We must have been within 10 yards of that exact spot several times during the previous 22 hours, but because of the tall grass, we just never saw it lying there," Steve said.

After the recovery, Steve noted that he'd made a perfect double-lung and heart shot. His arrow had done the trick, though the buck somehow managed to run about 160 yards before collapsing. Steve's 2009 trophy will share a place of honor in his basement with many of his other mounts, including another 203 3/8-inch buck taken in 1994.

Photo courtesy Steve Esker

Steve Esker Buck

Official Buckmasters Score Sheet		
Taken by:	**Steve Esker**	
Date:	**September 29, 2009**	
Location:	**Franklin Co., Ohio**	
Method:	**Crossbow**	
Classification:	**Irregular**	
Measurements:	**Right**	**Left**
Total Points Side	10	9
Irregular Points Side	5	4
Total Irregular Inches	16 3/8	9
Length of Main Beam	26	25 5/8
Length of 1st Point	3 7/8	6 5/8
Length of 2nd Point	14 4/8	13 6/8
Length of 3rd Point	9 5/8	12 2/8
Length of 4th Point	4 6/8	4 4/8
Length of 5th Point		
Length of 6th Point		
1st Circumference (C1)	6 5/8	6 3/8
2nd Circumference (C2)	6 2/8	6
3rd Circumference (C3)	5 2/8	5 2/8
4th Circumference (C4)	5 6/8	4 5/8
Score Per Side	99	94
OFFICIAL SCORE	193	
Inside Spread	19 2/8	
COMPOSITE SCORE	212 2/8	
Percentage of Irregularity	13.1%	

If Ever There Was an Omen
Todd Bailey Buck

Photo courtesy of Todd Bailey

Seeing a great buck with a doe while he was driving to his hunting spot on Nov. 5, 2009, primed Todd Bailey's pump. The deer were in a soccer field within a mile of his destination, and it wasn't even 3:00.

It was no ordinary buck either. Todd figured it for a 160-something-incher. And he couldn't wait to get into his ladder stand.

"That was my first year to hunt that little section and my third trip that season, though I'd acquired it several years earlier," he said. "It's a small 5-acre plot of woods and CRP, completely surrounded by croplands that had most recently held soybeans.

"I'd like to say that I had scouted the area extensively and had a good idea of what was likely to happen, but my holdings are very small. There's not much a guy can do besides hope," he added.

Todd wasn't going in completely blind, however. He knew the woodlot held a clearly defined rub line and several active scrapes. Even if they didn't live on his place, lots of deer – presumably some very good bucks, too – were passing through there.

"Seeing that big buck on the way to my stand had me pumped," he said. "I knew the rut was on, and the big ones obviously were moving during the daytime.

"I had been putting out some corn to attract does to my property, and I had also established a mineral lick near a natural spring that seeped steadily from the ground. The spring provided a good flow of water, summer and winter, and the deer frequented it. My ladder stand was near there," he continued.

In his first two sittings in '09, Todd had seen a pretty good 10-point buck and a doe, but they never came within crossbow range.

Todd was aloft by 3 p.m. Although the wind had lessened considerably and the temperature was in the low 50s, nothing was moving inside the woodlot.

"From my stand, I could see almost every square foot of the five acres and even into the fields beyond," he said. "There were a couple of good thickets I couldn't see into, but it was unlikely anything was in those since I'd walked right past them. I had a good vantage point, but if nothing is there to see, then there's nothing to shoot."

The silence continued for two hours.

"I was on the verge of getting down at 5:00 and going home when I spotted movement to my far right. When I focused on it, I realized it was a very nice, large-bodied buck. It was simply moseying along, seemingly without a care in the world.

"Before I climbed into my stand, I had sprinkled a bit of Tinks #69 nearby. Actually, I used half a bottle. The earlier winds had surely spread the scent around, and I couldn't help wondering if that was what brought that buck to my little patch of woods.

"The buck was coming toward me. If it stayed on course, it would pass within 25 to 30 yards. It kept coming, too – walking, stopping to sniff, and then walking again. I was sure it was locked onto the Tinks and thought it was following a doe," he said.

"After seeing the rack initially, I knew I could not look at it again. I had to concentrate only on shot placement. As the deer got closer, I raised my crossbow and prepared for the shot. I watched as the buck neared my 25-yard marker, and then I let it pass so it was quartering away from me.

"When it was just beyond 25 yards, I released the bolt. It looked like a very good hit just behind the left shoulder. I could actually see the wound," Todd continued.

The buck bolted maybe 40 yards before collapsing in the tall grass right in front of Todd. It might have kicked a couple of times, but then it went still.

"Just that quick, the hunt was over; it couldn't have been more than two minutes from my first seeing the buck 'till it was lying on the ground.

"When I was holding on the buck and ready to pull the trigger, this thought kept running through my mind: 'If I screw up and miss this buck, I will be devastated'

"I didn't wait any time at all before I got down because I could plainly see the buck was dead. After I lowered my gear, I walked straight over to it.

"Since I was hunting alone and there was nobody to share the excitement with me, there was no need to linger. I dressed it out, loaded it up and was on my way to the check station before dark.

"I knew there were deer in this area. Even though I'd owned the land for almost five years, I was just never in a position to hunt it until that week. I have talked to a lot of people who live around here, and they've all said there are a lot of big deer.

"It was really a strange day. I was low, at first,

because it was warm and windy. I saw nothing
before this incredible buck arrived. My elation was
very high at my success, and then it went low again
as there was no one present to share joy," he said.

Photo courtesy of Todd Bailey

Todd Bailey Buck

Official Buckmasters Score Sheet		
Taken by:	**Todd A. Bailey**	
Date:	**November 5, 2009**	
Location:	**Clark Co., Ohio**	
Method:	**Crossbow**	
Classification:	**Typical**	
Measurements:	**Right**	**Left**
Total Points Side	8	6
Irregular Points Side	2	1
Total Irregular Inches	5 3/8	1 5/8
Length of Main Beam	25 6/8	25 4/8
Length of 1st Point	5 7/8	9
Length of 2nd Point	10 4/8	11 4/8
Length of 3rd Point	12 1/8	11 7/8
Length of 4th Point	8 1/8	8 4/8
Length of 5th Point	2	
Length of 6th Point		
1st Circumference (C1)	5 3/8	5 3/8
2nd Circumference (C2)	4 7/8	4 5/8
3rd Circumference (C3)	5 4/8	4 6/8
4th Circumference (C4)	4 3/8	4 6/8
Score Per Side	89 7/8	87 4/8
OFFICIAL SCORE	177 3/8	
Inside Spread	21 5/8	
COMPOSITE SCORE	199	
Percentage of Irregularity	3.9%	

Same Stand, Same Day
Dad's Best, Son's First
Leonard Bakker Buck

Photo courtesy of Leonard Bakker

Ohio's 2009 gun season was rapidly winding down; it was Saturday with only Sunday remaining. The season had been pretty much a bust for Leonard Bakker and his son, Travis.

Leonard had set up a two-person treestand on 65 acres of private land in Clinton County in southwestern Ohio.

"I had taken off the whole week to hunt the gun season and, to be honest, it had been a disappointment," he said. "Saturday was going to be my son's second day (ever) of deer hunting and, at 11 years old, he was more than ready to get in the stand. I wasn't as enthusiastic, however, because I hadn't seen much activity there."

Travis had been given a new scoped, 20-gauge shotgun, and he'd been filling a cardboard deer target with holes. He was proficient out to 100 yards.

"We were in the double treestand well before daylight," Leonard said. "I was hoping we'd see deer right from the start, but nothing was happening.

"As time wore on, my son grew antsy. To keep him interested, we talked about how important it is to keep as still as possible and to communicate by whispering, only when necessary. We also decided we'd tap the other on the knee if we saw something, and then – instead of pointing – we'd use a clock system to describe where to look.

"About 8:00, a doe ran onto the field 80 yards distant. Since I was sitting on that side of the stand, I immediately shouldered my shotgun. I was a second away from squeezing the trigger when I spotted a big buck about 20 yards behind her. As soon as I switched targets, I fired.

"The buck jumped, bolted 40 yards, stumbled, and then it went head-first to the ground, doing a complete somersault," Leonard continued.

The doe was still running around, coming close to the downed buck, stomping, snorting and wheezing as she tried to figure out what happened to her suitor.

"I decided this would be a perfect shot for Travis, so I had him shoulder his gun and try to get on the doe. By the time he got set up for the shot, no easy feat because of all the excitement over the buck, the doe decided it was time to abandon loverboy.

"I told Travis that we'd stay in the tree for at least 30 minutes, although he was dying to get a closer look. After the minutes ticked by, we lowered our empty guns to the ground and got down," Leonard said.

The buck was a 12-pointer, a massive mainframe 3x3 with three extra points on each side (that contributed more than 50 inches to the BTR score).

"The first thing I did was to photograph it with my cell phone, and then I called my wife and brother. After sharing photos with them, I prepared and attached the tag and field-dressed the deer, which didn't bother Travis at all.

"When we tried dragging the deer out of the field, we realized it was way too big. I wound up driving my minivan onto the field, tying the buck to the bumper and dragging it out that way – with Travis following on footstep to make sure the rack did not get caught on anything.

"After getting it loaded on our trailer, we took off to get it officially tagged at Bill's Carryout near the Caesar's Creek Dam, and then it was off to a few friends' houses before heading home," Leonard said.

Father and son returned to the stand at 3:30 p.m.

"I carried my shotgun only because I still had a doe tag. But the first order of business was to get my son a deer," Leonard said. "I guess it was about 4:00 when Travis poked my leg and said, 'Dad, there's a deer at 10:30.'

"I thought he was fooling with the 10:30 stuff, but I focused my attention that way and, sure enough, saw a deer 200 yards across the field and heading our way.

"I told Travis to raise his gun and to get on the deer quickly, though it was too far to shoot with a 20 gauge. When the buck was about 140 yards away, I told Travis to take it," Leonard continued.

Travis missed, and then Leonard was frantically digging in his pockets for more shells. He wound up handing his own 12 gauge to his son. The boy missed twice more with his dad's gun.

"He said he was leading the slow-moving buck, but I told him he didn't need to worry about that," Leonard said.

The fourth shot connected. The buck jumped, and then ran about 60 yards before collapsing in the field.

"Travis was shaking like a leaf in a wind," Leonard said. "He told me, 'Dad, I'm really cold. I can't stop shaking.'

"I said, 'Son, that isn't cold. That is an adrenaline rush from all the excitement while trying to shoot your first buck. You'll be fine in a few minutes, and then we'll get down and go look at your deer.'"

Leonard & Travis Bakker Bucks

Official Buckmasters Score Sheet		
Taken by:	**Leonard Bakker**	
Date:	**December 5, 2009**	
Location:	**Clinton Co., Ohio**	
Method:	**Shotgun**	
Classification:	**Irregular**	
Measurements:	**Right**	**Left**
Total Points Side	6	6
Irregular Points Side	3	3
Total Irregular Inches	34 7/8	15 6/8
Length of Main Beam	22	23 6/8
Length of 1st Point	12 6/8	15 6/8
Length of 2nd Point	10 3/8	13 7/8
Length of 3rd Point		
Length of 4th Point		
Length of 5th Point		
Length of 6th Point		
1st Circumference (C1)	6 5/8	6 5/8
2nd Circumference (C2)	4 2/8	4 4/8
3rd Circumference (C3)	3 3/8	3 4/8
4th Circumference (C4)	2 5/8	3
Score Per Side	96 7/8	86 6/8
OFFICIAL SCORE	183 5/8	
Inside Spread	14	
COMPOSITE SCORE	197 5/8	
Percentage of Irregularity	27.5%	

Gene Pool
Two things are clear: Joe Harris' farm has big deer, and his children know how to shoot.
Paige Harris Buck

Photo courtesy J. Harris family

It's not for lack of trying that 10-year-old Joey Harris hasn't spent much time in front of a camera, at least not while wearing hunter orange and gripping a dead whitetail.

The boy came close last year, but the buck that would've landed him on the cover of this magazine just took the stage a little too late in the day and a bit too distant. He wanted to take a poke at it, but his dad, Joe, wouldn't let him.

If you're Joe Harris' kid, you might be able to skip school a time or two during Pennsylvania's too-short rifle season, but you don't take iffy shots.

There was nothing iffy about the distance or the light when the same buck showed the following morning, a Saturday, but Joey wasn't behind the gun. His sister, 14-year-old Paige, was sharing the stand with Joe.

Two things are abundantly clear: Joe Harris grows big deer on his 280-acre farm near Danville, Pa., and his children know how to shoot.

Two years ago, his oldest daughter, Hanna, shot a 16-pointer that wound up on the November 2011 cover of Rack magazine. That Northumberland County buck is the state's No. 1 Semi-irregular in the BTR's rifle category (its composite score is 209 2/8 inches).

Hanna was 16 when she shot her deer, the ninth largest ever felled in Penn's Woods.

Paige was hunting from the same stand when opportunity knocked in 2011.

The whole family knew about the 19-pointer long before Joey saw it at 150 yards in the fading daylight of Dec. 2. They suspected it was either the off spring or brother of the whitetail Hanna shot in 2010.

"The buck started to show up on trail cameras about mid September," Joe said. "It was also seen on other farms in the area."

When the 2011 rifle season opened on Monday, Nov. 28, almost a dozen family members were scattered over the Harris farm. Paige hunted with her mother, Maria, while Joe took Joey.

"Neither my wife nor I carry a gun when we are in a stand with the kids," he said. "We devote all our attention to helping them with their hunts."

Paige's day ended early because of basketball practice. She's on the team at Danville Middle School. It was Wednesday before she could return to the stand.

"I skipped half a day of school so I could hunt," she said. "We went out early. Dad and I sat in Mommy's stand — the one Hanna had sat in the previous year — but we saw only a few does."

Thursday night, when the family was returning home from a late indoor soccer match, the big buck from the trail camera photos crossed the driveway in front of their car. The whole family got to see it from just 25 yards.

Joey skipped school to hunt the next morning, but he was back in the classroom that afternoon.

After school, because Paige had more basketball practice, he and his father returned to the stand.

"Just before dark, we saw the buck at 150 yards," Joe said. "Joey wanted to take the shot, but I felt it was too far, and the light was very poor. After I took a look through the scope, I decided Joey wouldn't be shooting that night."

Saturday, Dec. 3, was Paige's turn.

"Dad and I were up early and out to the stand well before daylight," she said. "It was quiet in the woods when, just after sunrise, we saw a couple of does off to our left. We watched them as they moved around, while still keeping an eye on the rest of the field. About 8:00, two more does appeared to the right side of an oak flat. We watched them carefully, as they were acting kind of nervous, like something else was nearby.

"A few minutes later, this buck came out of the pines and into some hardwoods thick with saplings. It was leaving through the saplings, heading for the open oaks," she continued. "It was about 120 yards away and headed nearly straight toward us. I was using a shooting rest and was ready for any clear shot. When I thought I had the right angle, I squeezed my .243's trigger."

"I was watching through the binoculars when Paige fired, and I saw the buck hunch up as it turned and bounded off," Joe said. "By the time it had gone 20 yards, it was out of sight. I was pretty sure she'd hit the buck, but I couldn't pinpoint

174

where. So we sat, waited and talked."

The does that were with the buck were in no hurry to leave, so father and daughter watched them until they finally vanished. That's when Joe got down while Paige kept a watchful eye in case the buck reappeared.

When Joe reached where he thought the deer had been standing, he started to look for sign.

"I knew I was close, and then I found some blood," he said. "I tracked back a few yards until I found some white hair, and then walked a few yards in the direction the deer had fled. There was blood, but not as much as I would've liked. I had a gut feeling the shot had been too far back, so I returned to the stand. We decided to go back to the house and gather a support team."

"We called pretty much everybody we knew who was hunting on the farm that day and explained what happened and what we planned to do that afternoon,"

Paige took up the tale. "We wanted everyone to spread out in a circle along the woods where we thought the deer might've gone, and then Dad and I were going to start following the blood trail and see where it went.

"When everyone was in position, we started following the sign. I don't think we went very far before I saw the buck bedded down on a logging road. I told Dad, 'There it is, there it is!' Then dad saw it and said, 'Shoot! Shoot!' And I did!"

"When I first saw the buck, it was almost curled up in a ball," Joe said. "It appeared to be weak, but it got up and started to walk away. That's when I started telling Paige to shoot. It was probably only 25 yards away.

"She made a good shot, and the buck went down, and I mean DOWN. It was right at the edge of a steep drop and, when it fell, slid all the way to the bottom. Fortunately, there's another logging road down there. That made retrieving it easier.

"I got a little excited after that," Joe continued. "While attempting to unload my gun, I jammed it. I told Paige to get on down there and, if the deer started to move, shoot it again."

"As soon as I got down to the buck, I started counting points," Paige said.

"When Dad finally got to me, we celebrated with high-fives and a hug before calling the rest of the gang. I stayed with the buck while Dad went back to the house for the four-wheeler. By the time he returned, several family members were there with me, and we continued to celebrate all the way back to the garage," she said.

Photo courtesy J. Harris family

Paige Harris Buck

Official Buckmasters Score Sheet		
Taken by:	**Paige Harris**	
Date:	**December 3, 2011**	
Location:	**Northumberland, PA**	
Method:	**Modern Rifle**	
Classification:	**Irregular**	
Measurements:	**Right**	**Left**
Total Points Side	**10**	**9**
Irregular Points Side	**5**	**4**
Total Irregular Inches	**13 6/8**	**12**
Length of Main Beam	**24 5/8**	**23 6/8**
Length of 1st Point	**7**	**8 7/8**
Length of 2nd Point	**11**	**8 1/8**
Length of 3rd Point	**11**	**9 2/8**
Length of 4th Point	**4 4/8**	**4 6/8**
Length of 5th Point		
Length of 6th Point		
1st Circumference (C1)	**5 4/8**	**5 4/8**
2nd Circumference (C2)	**4 4/8**	**4 5/8**
3rd Circumference (C3)	**4 3/8**	**4 1/8**
4th Circumference (C4)	**3 6/8**	**3 5/8**
Score Per Side	**90**	**84 5/8**
OFFICIAL SCORE	**174 5/8**	
Inside Spread	**23 5/8**	
COMPOSITE SCORE	**198 2/8**	
Percentage of Irregularity	**14.7%**	

Fourteen Pointer Runs Out of Luck

Spencer Forsythe Buck

Photo courtesy Spencer Forsythe

"I can't believe you missed it," Kyle Forsythe told his son, Spencer.

"I'm sorry," the boy replied.

"I just can't believe you missed it."

"I'm sorry I missed it."

"You don't have to apologize. It's just a once-in-a-lifetime opportunity, and you missed it."

"Look, I said I was sorry, alright?"

Kyle and Spencer, relative newcomers to deer hunting, were staring at the empty woodlot where, moments earlier, a huge buck had stood. The boy was the first to see and shoot at it. His dad had even taken a Hail-Mary at the fleeing animal, which looked perfectly healthy when it was turning on the afterburners.

After a few minutes had passed, Kyle realized the ridiculousness of berating his son. He was suffering as much from buck fever as was his charge, and he began chuckling, which also was contagious.

"We laughed at that silly conversation," Kyle said. "And after we settled down a bit, we decided to get down and see if we could find any blood. It was getting late anyway."

Kyle knew his son could handle the .243 Winchester, so they had to check. In the three seasons since they'd both taken the hunter safety course so Spencer could try his hand at the sport his older brother, Ryan, loved, the youngster had taken two bucks and a doe, all on opening day, all between 3:30 and 4:30.

The Forsythes own 85 acres in rural Jefferson County, Pa. Hunting rates a distant third behind trail riding with dirt bikes, ATVs and mountain bikes.

Two hundred yards behind their home, Ryan built a 20-foot-high platform within a cluster of five mature maple trees overlooking a clearing within the hardwoods. That's where Kyle and Spencer sat on Nov. 30, opening day of the 2009 rifle season, which is as much a holiday as the earlier Thanksgiving.

Prior to the season, rumors of a huge buck were circulating, which had Spencer pumped. The boy was the first in his family to confirm the gossip.

"About two weeks before the opener, I was looking out the dining room window and noticed a very large buck come out of the woods near the house. I thought no one would believe me, so I grabbed my camera and photographed it," he said. "We were sure it was the deer everyone was referring to because it was much bigger than anything else we'd seen."

From that moment on, Spencer frequently announced that he was going to shoot the deer.

Father and son watched the sunrise from the platform on opening day, despite the sporadic misting rain. It was cold, but not enough to snow.

"It was a slow day as hunting goes," Kyle said. "We heard very few shots from the surrounding hills and valleys. The deer were just not moving."

Spencer decided midmorning he'd go back to the house, warm up and eat. Kyle stayed in the stand. When the boy returned about 10:00, his dad was ready for a change of scenery.

"I got down and decided to circle through the woods to see if I could run a deer back toward

181

Spencer," he said. "As I was making my way along, I saw a bobcat. I had never seen one in the wild before. When I got back to the treestand, Spencer said he hadn't seen anything while I was gone."

After another hour passed, Spencer went to the house. He came back out at 3:00.

"After a while, I could tell he was getting bored again. He was shuffling around and not paying enough attention," Kyle said. "I thought if we traded places and he could watch a different part of the clearing, he might perk up a bit. So we shifted.

"Two or three minutes later, I heard Spencer say, 'It's a buck,' and I turned to look. I saw only half the rack, at first, but it was absolutely huge," Kyle said. "I whispered to Spencer, 'If you get that thing in your scope, don't wait. Just squeeze the trigger as soon as you can. Don't wait for it to turn or get closer. Just take the first shot.'"

The deer was 80 yards distant and getting closer.

"I had a good view of the deer as it was coming right toward us," Spencer said. "It was moving pretty quickly. I had my rifle up and was getting ready to squeeze the trigger when I heard Dad whisper for me to shoot. Just then, the buck raised its head and looked straight at me.

"A split second later, I fired straight into the front of its neck and chest," he continued. "All I could remember was the lines in the scope moving around in a circle on the front of the deer as I squeezed the trigger. I hoped it was in a good spot when the gun fired."

The deer spun around and took off running.

"I also had my new open-sighted rifle to my shoulder in case we needed a follow-up shot," Kyle said. "I tried, but the deer was moving too fast. I missed."

After regaining their senses, Kyle and Spencer went to look for blood. They were thrilled when they came across some. Kyle decided that since neither he nor Spencer were experienced trackers, they needed help. Spencer called two friends, who were hunting nearby, and a neighbor.

Not long after he finished the calls, Spencer bent down and peered through the trees along the trail the buck had taken. He saw what looked like a broken tree limb he didn't remember being there earlier, so he called his dad over to investigate.

"When I bent down to look under the overhanging branches, I saw the dead buck. It had gone about 100 yards," Kyle said.

"The 18-year-old neighbor boy arrived a few minutes later. He told us he'd seen that deer earlier and had his gun on it, but he was shaking too badly to take the shot," Kyle added. "We also learned after the fact that another hunter encountered the same deer earlier in the day and had actually missed it on the other side of the hill from us.

"I guess its luck ran out when it wandered into Spencer's sights."

Photo courtesy Spencer Forsythe

Spencer Forsythe Buck

Official Buckmasters Score Sheet		
Taken by:	**Spencer Forsythe**	
Date:	**November 30, 2009**	
Location:	**Jefferson Co., PA**	
Method:	**Modern Rifle**	
Classification:	**Semi-Irregular**	
Measurements:	**Right**	**Left**
Total Points Side	7	7
Irregular Points Side	3	2
Total Irregular Inches	8 3/8	8 6/8
Length of Main Beam	24 4/8	24 7/8
Length of 1st Point	7 1/8	8 4/8
Length of 2nd Point	10 7/8	10 7/8
Length of 3rd Point	9 4/8	10 2/8
Length of 4th Point		4 6/8
Length of 5th Point		
Length of 6th Point		
1st Circumference (C1)	5 5/8	5 7/8
2nd Circumference (C2)	5 5/8	5 5/8
3rd Circumference (C3)	5 3/8	5 1/8
4th Circumference (C4)	4 5/8	4 5/8
Score Per Side	81 5/8	89 2/8
OFFICIAL SCORE	170 7/8	
Inside Spread	19	
COMPOSITE SCORE	189 7/8	
Percentage of Irregularity	10.0%	

What a Difference 668 Days Make
Troy Johnson Buck

Photo courtesy Troy Johnson

It's probably a good thing Troy Johnson's luck wasn't so good in 2008.

Ditto for 2009.

While the Ohio bowhunter would've been very happy to stick a 165-inch whitetail in 2008, or the same deer -- only 25 inches bigger -- in 2009, doing so would've robbed him of being one of 2010's inductees into the BTR 200 Club. Plus, his story would've fit on a business card.

Instead, you're reading it here.

Troy's first and only encounter with the buck in 2008 came during the season's final hunt. It was early January, when hunting over food sources is perhaps the best way to punch a tag.

Before that day, he had no idea such a buck was passing through the 12-acre woodlot he's hunted for 18 years.

"I was in a tree about 25 yards from a bait pile," he said. "Eight or 10 deer were feeding there, off and on, all afternoon, but none piqued my interest.

"Just before dark, I noticed a big buck standing downwind and about 100 yards due east of me. I watched it through my binoculars for several minutes," Troy continued. "I judged its rack to be about 165 inches -- a good buck, for sure. But it must have sensed something was wrong.

"Even though other deer were feeding between us, it would not come any closer," he said.

The following summer, Troy began retrieving trail camera photos of the buck. He had several units stashed in the woods, which flank more than 1,000 acres of marsh and a CRP field. Croplands about the far side.

Most of the photos were taken at a well

established mineral lick.

"It had to be the same buck, only bigger ... closer to 190 inches," explained the hunter.

"Oct. 12 was the first time I was able to hunt in 2009," Troy said. "I was in a row of trees between the marsh and the CRP field. It was really more of a scouting trip. I wanted to get an idea of what was going on out there, to see where and when the deer were crossing and if the big buck might show during daylight.

"I was in the tree by 2 p.m.," he continued. "About an hour later, this buck stood up from its bed 100 yards out in the CRP. That was the second time I had actually seen the deer with my own eyes.

"It stood there looking around in every direction for at least 10 minutes, and then, when it decided all was clear, it bedded back down in the same spot.

"Of course, I had tunnel vision during the rest of the afternoon," Troy said.

The buck remained in its bed until only 30 minutes before dark. When it finally stood, it looked around and began ambling toward the woods.

"I immediately grunted a few times, and it turned and started coming toward me," Troy said. "It hung up at about 50 yards, however. It was directly upwind and couldn't smell me, but it refused to come closer."

"That distance would've been okay for me, but I was not about to try it under windy conditions. Plus, this buck was too incredible to risk a marginal shot.

"I tried every trick in my bag to lure it closer, but to no avail," he continued. "The buck wandered off, disappearing into the shadows, which is why I nicknamed him the Gray Ghost."

Troy has no idea what caused the buck to leave him that day, and that was only time he saw it in 2009.

The next August (2010), Troy set out his trail cameras and checked them every week. He was thrilled to retrieve a photo of the buck at his mineral lick.

"Between August and October, I got more than 100 pictures of the buck, mostly at night," he said. "He had grown substantially from the previous year; I guessed he'd score well into the 200s, perhaps even 250. He looked like an elk when in velvet."

It's no wonder Troy decided to devote the season to finding that buck in his sights. He had three stands that allowed him to hunt with the wind.

"There was a good acorn crop that year," he said. "I hunted while the nuts were dropping, but I never saw him. Then I hunted the stand overlooking the crop field's edge on the western side of the woods.

"After my hunt on Oct. 29, I pulled the chip from a camera overlooking a major trail bordering the CRP. I had two daylight pictures of him dogging a doe the previous day," he added. "Those were the first daylight shots I'd gotten in two years!"

Despite his intention to hunt the entire day, Troy had to work the next morning. He didn't get into his CRP stand until almost noon.

"There was a strong west-southwesterly wind of about 20 mph, and I wanted to be on the opposite side of the woods from where the trail camera had photographed him two days earlier," he said.

Between 1:30 and 2:00, a big mature doe approached in a trot from downwind. She stood beneath Troy for 10 or 15 minutes, and then she settled down and went back out into the CRP, bedding down just 40 yards from him.

"I kept a watchful eye on her," Troy said.

He didn't see another deer until 5:15, and it was the Gray Ghost skirting the edge of the woods.

"He was heading right for that hot doe," he said. "It was incredible to watch. The buck was grunting, thrashing trees with his antlers, stopping to paw the ground, peeing on his hocks ... just tearing up the edge line as he came closer.

"I tried grunting a few times to make him think another buck was close, but he never paid me any attention. I thought he would never be in range as he came around, but when he was directly downwind of me, he stopped and stood for several minutes, checking the air and pawing the ground.

"Suddenly, the doe jumped up from her bed and went directly south. My high vantage point gave me a clear view of the entire field. He might not have seen her for the tall growth, but I am sure he heard her making an exit.

"Almost instantly, the buck was following her across the field. But he made one very fatal mistake: He stopped broadside at 47 yards to check her scent.

"I threaded my arrow (bolt) through a small opening in a pin oak tree and made the perfect shot," he said.

The buck ran only 30 yards across the CRP, and

then stopped and laid down. Within minutes, he was finished.

"That was the shortest hunting season I've ever had, but, oh, what a season!" Troy said.

"I'm not a new kid on the block. I've heard all the stories about hunters killing big bucks and battling rumors. To nip that in the bud, I called the local game warden, who was happy to come out and take a look."

The officer verified where the buck was shot and where it fell. He even put the metal band on the antlers to certify that it had been checked-in.

Photo courtesy Troy Johnson

Troy Johnson Buck

Official Buckmasters Score Sheet		
Taken by:	**Troy Johnson**	
Date:	**October 30, 2010**	
Location:	**Sandusky Co., Ohio**	
Method:	**Crossbow**	
Classification:	**Irregular**	
Measurements:	**Right**	**Left**
Total Points Side	13	10
Irregular Points Side	6	3
Total Irregular Inches	26 2/8	9 2/8
Length of Main Beam	26 1/8	26
Length of 1st Point	6 3/8	8 2/8
Length of 2nd Point	10 4/8	10 4/8
Length of 3rd Point	10 2/8	10 1/8
Length of 4th Point	8 6/8	10 4/8
Length of 5th Point	3	7 3/8
Length of 6th Point		3
1st Circumference (C1)	5 6/8	5
2nd Circumference (C2)	4 6/8	4 5/8
3rd Circumference (C3)	4 6/8	4 5/8
4th Circumference (C4)	6 6/8	5 7/8
Score Per Side	113 2/8	105 1/8
OFFICIAL SCORE	218 3/8	
Inside Spread	20 2/8	
COMPOSITE SCORE	238 5/8	
Percentage of Irregularity	16.2%	

Squirrel's-Eye View
Widow takes late husband's advice, climbs rungs
for chance at photogenic whitetail.
Nikki Bechtel Buck

Photo courtesy of Nikki Bechtel

Unlike the dinosaurs in the "Jurassic Park" movies, unlike the great white shark in "Jaws," and unlike the brawls between TV's professional wrestlers (with apologies to believers), the buck whose photograph appeared on Shawn and Nikki Bechtel's trail camera in 2011 was very real.

Husband and wife —- it was she who taught him how to hunt — were instantly smitten with the deer they named Bullwinkle. Shawn had more time than his wife, and he had a slight advantage because he bowhunted from treestands. Nikki, afraid of heights, always hunted from ground blinds.

Nikki's time afield was mostly during weekends, since her drive home from work didn't allow any time for late—afternoon sits.

Regardless of how much time the two of them spent waiting, separately or together, Bullwinkle never once appeared while the sun was overhead. Not in 2011; not in 2012.

Shawn would not get to hunt in 2013, and Nikki lost her enthusiasm for it.

"My husband died in January of a serious and ongoing heart condition, and I nearly gave up hunting after that," she said.

Nevertheless, she left their trail cameras in the field, and she continued to monitor them — more out of habit than interest.

"It just seemed like the right thing to do," she said. "I knew my husband wanted me to get a crack at that buck. He even urged me to use his ladder stand when he got to the point he could no longer go into the woods."

"At the time, though, I didn't seem to have the time or the inclination to be out there alone," Nikki added.

Seven months later, in August, Bullwinkle's distinctive mug began reappearing on camera. Nikki says she collected maybe 50 photos of the deer from all angles.

"It was like he was taunting me," she said.

"After looking at the pictures many times, I noticed a white, gauzy apparition in a few of the shots. It did not appear in all of the photos, but in enough to cause me to wonder."

"I believe in spirits," she says matter-of—factly. "I believe my husband's spirit was trying to tell me I needed to get my life back on track."

"Several years earlier, Shawn urged me to pursue my dream of becoming a taxidermist. With his encouragement, I started Woods to Wall Taxidermy," she continued. "When Shawn's heart problem became very serious, I wanted to quit the taxidermy business and even my job just to be with him, but he made me promise to keep going and to make my dream come true."

"I can't forget what happened on the day of his funeral. I received a call from a hunter who wanted to know if I would do his deer mount. I was right on the verge of saying no when something inside me said 'Do it, girl!' And I did. I accepted his deer," Nikki said.

"If the spirit moves you, and you believe in spirits, you go where you are told to go," she added.

After ogling all the photographs of Bullwinkle near her ground blind, and remembering how much Shawn had wanted her to try his ladder to be above the deer's line of scent, Nikki began considering the very thing that terrified her most. She wound up buying a two—person ladder stand.

"Granted, it was only 16 feet tall, but it certainly was a start," she said. "I had a few of our friends help me put it in place, and even climbed up one time while the guys were there to help get me back down if panicked."

"I really never thought I would have the nerve to get up there when I was alone," she continued.

The steady stream of photographs stopped on Oct. 19. Nikki hadn't hunted yet, despite friends Timmy and Danny urging her to get out there.

"I awoke one Sunday morning with no thoughts of going hunting, even though I knew my friends would all be out there. As the day progressed, however, something kept after me to get myself out of the house and into the woods," she said.

"It was early afternoon when I finally made the decision to gear up and go. I went directly to my favorite spot. I wasn't going to climb the ladder; I was going to sit in the nearby ground blind."

"But I hesitated and remembered what Shawn had said, 'If you want a crack at this buck, you are going to have to get up above him!' And so I climbed, shaking, into the stand and strapped myself in," she continued.

"So many thoughts were running through my head at the time. I had not told anyone I was going hunting, not even my parents, so if something happened, no one would have a clue to look for me. I was becoming quite nervous sitting there, since it was a whole new experience for me."

"In order to calm my nerves, I took out my cell phone and began playing Bejeweled. It seemed to relax me, and I wasn't quite so conscious of the elevation," she added.

Close to 4:15, Nikki heard a ruckus in the deep ravine behind her. It didn't sound like deer or squirrels; just noise. And then it grew distant and stopped altogether.

"Maybe 20 or 30 minutes later, I glanced around and saw a huge buck underneath me," she said. "I remembered everyone telling me, 'Once you see the big rack, don't stare. Look for the target, for an opening, and plan your shot.'"

"I immediately grabbed my crossbow and started looking for an opening as the buck was moving away at a right-to-left angle. It was 38 to 40 yards away from me when it finally stepped into a clear lane and I took the quartering shot," she continued. "It jumped big time, and then took off running. I wasn't sure whether I hit it or not, but I kept telling myself it was a good shot."

Turns out, she'd judged the distance correctly.

"I sat there for quite a while before I got down, too excited to worry about the height. I immediately began texting my friends to get help," she said. "I had never shot a deer before, nor had I ever tracked one. And it was a sure bet I wouldn't be able to drag it out on my own."

"No one was responding to my texts, so I was starting to get uncomfortable. I'm screaming in my head, Come on, SOMEONE, ANYONE, text me back. I need help!"

The noise Nikki heard in the ravine earlier was Timmy dragging out a deer he'd shot. He was too busy to check his texts.

"While I waited, I began looking for and found the arrow, which was covered in blood," she said.

Finally, her phone buzzed with a reply from Timmy. It was a great relief to know he and Danny were coming to lend a hand.

Eventually her friends arrived in the woods and the search began in earnest. Danny found the buck about 160 yards from where she shot it. He looked at Nikki afterward and stated quite bluntly, "You shot him. It's him alright. It's him!"

"What do you mean, it's him?" she asked.

"You shot him. It's Bullwinkle, and you just shot him," he replied.

"I started screaming and ran over and kissed Danny and then I ran over kissed Timmy. I looked at both and then told them that Shawn brought him to me. My angel was right there beside me in that stand."

"Then I ran over and jumped on my deer. It was a very, very emotional moment for me as tears came to my eyes."

"I called home after that. I had to tell my dad I had taken Bullwinkle. I don't think he believed me until my excitement boiled over, and then he was as excited as I was."

Photo courtesy of Nikki Bechtel

Nikki Bechtel Buck

Official Buckmasters Score Sheet		
Taken by:	Nikki Gasbarre-Bechtel	
Date:	November 24, 2013	
Location:	Warren Co., Ohio	
Method:	Crossbow	
Classification:	Irregular	
Measurements:	Right	Left
Total Points Side	11	8
Irregular Points Side	6	2
Total Irregular Inches	23 7/8	13 7/8
Length of Main Beam	22	23
Length of 1st Point	5 2/8	6 5/8
Length of 2nd Point	11 1/8	11 5/8
Length of 3rd Point	10	10
Length of 4th Point	6 3/8	10 3/8
Length of 5th Point		5 2/8
Length of 6th Point		
1st Circumference (C1)	5 6/8	5 6/8
2nd Circumference (C2)	4 3/8	4 2/8
3rd Circumference (C3)	5	5 7/8
4th Circumference (C4)	4 3/8	5 7/8
Score Per Side	98 1/8	102 4/8
OFFICIAL SCORE	200 5/8	
Inside Spread	17 1/8	
COMPOSITE SCORE	217 6/8	
Percentage of Irregularity	18.8%	

OH, Brother
Mike Smith Buck

Photo by Ed Waite

Brothers Mike and Tim Smith pair up each season to hunt a 50-acre hardwood section in Greene County, Ohio. Mike, who lives near Detroit, takes time off from work in the fall and drives the three-hour stretch down I-75 most Thursday evenings to his brother's house.

In 2009, he and his brother had set up their stands beside deer trails in what they call a "transitional" woodlot surrounded by farm fields. Heavily trodden trails, rubs and scrapes litter the property.

"It was mid-November, probably the fourth straight weekend I had been down there to hunt," Mike said. "On Saturday evening, as we were discussing the next morning's hunt, my brother decided he would go to church. I would hunt by myself."

"I like to get in the woods really early. By 6 a.m., I was situated in Tim's stand, which overlooks an old tractor path circling the woodlot. His seemed to have the most morning traffic. The temperature was in the mid-40s, and there was no wind. It was dead quiet in the woods until everything started waking up around 7:00."

"At 7:30, I saw something moving about 40 yards down the trail. A small 7-pointer was following the tractor path with its head down, coming straight toward me. It passed under the stand and was gone in about three minutes," Mike continued.

"I usually tell my brother about everything I see and when so we can keep track of all the activity. After the 7-pointer disappeared, I resumed watching the antics of squirrels. About 8:00, I heard a loud racket behind me and turned slightly to look over my left shoulder. An absolute monster was at 40 yards, coming down the trail at a pretty good clip."

"I could see tell the rack was huge and wide, and that's all I really needed to know."

"The problem was that I'm a lefty and was sitting down in my brother's right-hand stand. My bow was on the wrong side, and I needed to turn and reach across my body to get it off the hook."

"That buck was so close and coming in so quickly, I didn't dare try standing to make the shot. The deer was inside of 20 yards when I lifted my bow off the hook, barely clipping the hanger. I glanced sideways and saw the buck – 5 yards away – stop and stare at the tree. Thankfully, it never looked up at me."

"I thought the game was over, but the buck just turned slightly and began slowly walking. It was quartering away at about 18 yards on my strong side when I got my pin on its shoulder and released the arrow. I saw it enter and heard the thwack of broadhead hitting the opposite shoulder," Mike continued.

"The buck jumped pretty high and to the right before it tore out of there. It bulldozed over some small trees, which pulled out the arrow, and then it was gone."

"I started to get all shaky and flushed with excitement. The whole thing had taken less than three minutes," he said.

"I sat there for several minutes, replaying the scene in my mind, and then I finally picked up the phone to call my brother. When he answered, he said, 'What's up?'"

"I'm going to need your help," I said.

"Why's that?"

"I got a big one."

"You got a big one?"

"Yep, I think it's pretty big ... at least a mainframe 10-pointer and more. But I couldn't see everything because I didn't have a lot of time to put the glasses on it."

"Did you put a good shot on it?"

"I think so."

"Alright. Just sit tight. I'm on my way."

"I put the phone away and sat for a while to calm down before trying to descend the tree," he said. "I walked over to where I thought the deer had gone into the underbrush, and there was no sign of my arrow. When I pictured those last few seconds, I remembered the buck veering right, and then I found half the shaft in a pool of blood."

"I followed the trail. Strangely, the buck seemed to have stopped at every rub and scrape, leaving a small pool of blood before moving on to the next. I eventually lost track of where I was in relation to the stand, but I knew I was closing in on the deer. I could smell it."

"When I came across another trail, I wondered if it might be heading toward land I wasn't sure we could access. I called my brother again. He asked me if I knew where I was, and I told him I was on a trail in Ohio, and that's all I knew."

"A little shook-up, are ya?" he laughed.

"Yes. All I know is this big boy is down. I can smell it, but I haven't found it yet."

"I'm getting out of the truck right now," Tim said. "I'll be there soon, so try to sit tight."

"I stayed where I was because there was a big puddle of blood right in the middle of the trail. When I heard my brother coming toward me, I stood up and walked a bit toward him. I was maybe 15 yards off the perimeter trail. If I had taken the time to look, I could've seen the stand I'd sat in the previous night. That's how focused I was on tracking."

As Tim came up to Mike, he said, "You're right. I can smell it, too. It's definitely rutted up, close and not moving … got to be down."

"My brother followed the blood trail, and I walked off to the side. We hadn't gone 15 yards before I saw the buck and yelled. We ran up to it together."

"I don't mind you shooting bucks out of my stand,' Tim told me. 'But did you have to shoot one this big?"

"We started laughing and carrying on like kids before photographing it and dragging it to the tractor path," Mike said.

Photo by Ed Waite

Official Buckmasters Score Sheet		
Taken by:	Mike Smith	
Date:	November 15, 2009	
Location:	Greene Co., Ohio	
Method:	Compound Bow	
Classification:	Irregular	
Measurements:	Right	Left
Total Points Side	11	9
Irregular Points Side	6	4
Total Irregular Inches	12 6/8	14 2/8
Length of Main Beam	25 5/8	24 4/8
Length of 1st Point	7	7 4/8
Length of 2nd Point	10 3/8	11 6/8
Length of 3rd Point	11	10 5/8
Length of 4th Point	9 4/8	5 7/8
Length of 5th Point		
Length of 6th Point		
1st Circumference (C1)	5 6/8	5 6/8
2nd Circumference (C2)	4 5/8	4 5/8
3rd Circumference (C3)	5 1/8	4 2/8
4th Circumference (C4)	4 3/8	3 7/8
Score Per Side	96 1/8	93
OFFICIAL SCORE	189 1/8	
Inside Spread	19	
COMPOSITE SCORE	208 1/8	
Percentage of Irregularity	14.2%	

Two-For-One Buck
Marion Goodpaster Buck

Photo courtesy of Marion Goodpaster

Marion Goodpaster was enjoying his ringside seat during last year's snot-slinging contest, but he really wanted it to end before the curtain fell on his Nov. 11 hunt in Ripley County, Ind.

The hunter from Aurora, Ind., was between a belligerent buck and an equally mouthy doe, both determined to send the other running for cover. Had it not been for another doe come to see what all the fuss was about, Marion might've gone stark raving mad.

He can blame — and thank — his son-in-law for putting him in the middle of the not-so-domestic dispute.

Marion was hunting his son-in- law's parents' 43-acre farm. After the first day afield, during which he'd found the perfect scrape and nearby tree, only to be forced to choose an alternate setup because of high winds, he called that night to ask more questions about the property.

"My son-in-law advised me to move farther into the woods, to follow a logging road and to look for a thicket where a nice 10-pointer had been killed the previous year," he said.

"I went in again about 10:30 the next morning and scouted along the logging road. I went down over the hill, which was exactly as he'd described, and found a really nice deer trail," he added.

Marion eventually came across a large scrape, recently tended, and decided to look for a suitable tree to climb on the adjacent hillside. He could still picture the huge 8-pointer he'd seen working a scrape the previous day.

He'd taken only a few steps toward the hill when he glanced to his left and saw a very nice 6-pointer staring at him from just 20 yards away.

"I was holding my crossbow, and my climber was strapped to my back," he said. "The most I could do before it bolted was to slip off the safety."

When the deer left, Marion resumed his quest for the perfect tree. It was going on noon by the time he'd found one and jacked himself up 20 feet.

"While surveying my surroundings, I saw another buck coming over the top of the hill from behind me. It was a big-bodied 4-pointer, but with some mass to it, maybe even some short brow tines," he said. "It cut across the hill toward the scrape I'd found the previous day."

"After it left, I decided to go to the house for a quick lunch and a bathroom break," he continued. "I wanted to scout some more, too, so I crossed over the hill and went down into the next hollow."

"I found even more scrapes, some very torn-up trees and was busted by another deer," Marion said. "After that, I went back to the house."

He returned to the farm about 4:00 and climbed the tree overlooking the scrape.

"I didn't see much of anything the first hour. But then I heard something coming from the same direction I'd just walked," he said. "It was a doe about 150 yards away. I watched her for a few minutes until she disappeared into the hollow, and then I saw a second, smaller doe.

"The little one came right to me," he added. "Knowing the rut was underway, I was wondering when I was going to see a buck." Soon, a third doe appeared and dipped into the hollow where the first one went. The yearling, meanwhile, was feeding right under Marion's stand.

"By 5:30, the sun was getting very low and shooting light was beginning to fade," he said. "I was really enjoying watching the yearling. But then I saw movement in the thicket about 100 yards away. There were two big-bodied deer out there, and one was wearing a huge rack."

"Eventually, the big buck jumped over a fallen tree and was outside the thicket, almost in the wide open, and staring in my direction," he continued. "I could tell the buck had a double beam on the right side, but it was too far away for me to consider taking a shot with my crossbow."

Although the wind was blowing in Marion's face, which meant the buck couldn't smell him, the deer hung up well beyond range and began stomping and snorting.

"I wasn't sure if it had spotted me or the yearling," Marion said.

"After a few more minutes of carrying on, the buck squatted real low, grunted loudly, and then stood and started making a scrape. When it finished pawing, it stepped forward and peed down its hocks and onto the bared ground," he said. "That was amazing to see, but things got even more surreal when the sun sank below the horizon."

"The yearling left, which was a relief. I was able to move a little. The buck took a few steps toward the hollow where the does were still feeding. It was as if it didn't want to go to them, but wanted them to come to it. One did come closer, at least."

"The buck seemed to be watching both her and me. I think it knew I was up the tree, but it didn't quite know what to make of me," he said. "Not to ease matters, the doe began stomping and snorting, too."

"The buck was at 60 yards at that point, moving slowly closer. Between us were two fairly large trees, one at 20 yards and the other at 30. I just hoped it would keep coming, and I decided to lift the crossbow as soon as the buck passed behind either one," he added.

Buck and doe were stomping and pawing the ground at each other, when the other doe came up over the hill, heading straight for Marion. When the buck noticed her, it started getting really agitated. And when the first doe saw her, she went berserk.

"Ultimately, the buck tried to run off the second doe, a maneuver that brought it even closer," Marion said. "I lifted my crossbow and tried to adjust to the scope, which actually improved the light. I then aimed and fired, and it looked like I double-lunged the buck, which raced up the hill to where I couldn't see it."

"I did hear a loud wheeze, however, before everything went quiet. That helped convince me it was on the ground —- 30 minutes after I'd first seen it," he added.

Even so, Marion was a nervous wreck. He'd never seen such a buck, and he'd never shot one with a crossbow. His had been a combination birthday-Christmas gift from his wife, Katee.

"As soon as I got down, I found the bloody arrow by using the light from my phone. After sticking it in the ground, I went back to my truck and retrieved my flashlight. I also called my son-in-law and his father to solicit their help.

"When I returned to the woods, I followed the trail for about 70 yards to my buck," he said. "I'm sure glad I called for help getting it out of there."

Photo courtesy of Marion Goodpaster

Marion Goodpaster Buck

216

Official Buckmasters Score Sheet		
Taken by: Date: Location: Method: Classification:	**Marion Goodpaster** **November 11, 2012** **Ripley Co., Indiana** **Crossbow** **Irregular**	
Measurements:	**Right**	Left
Total Points Side	9	7
Irregular Points Side	5	1
Total Irregular Inches	38 6/8	7 2/8
Length of Main Beam	21 7/8	27 5/8
Length of 1st Point	4 2/8	3 3/8
Length of 2nd Point	8 2/8	12 4/8
Length of 3rd Point	8 2/8	10 2/8
Length of 4th Point		1 4/8
Length of 5th Point		
Length of 6th Point		
1st Circumference (C1)	6	4 5/8
2nd Circumference (C2)	3 5/8	4 1/8
3rd Circumference (C3)	3 3/8	4 6/8
4th Circumference (C4)	2 6/8	4 6/8
Score Per Side	97 1/8	80 6/8
OFFICIAL SCORE	177 7/8	
Inside Spread	21 2/8	
COMPOSITE SCORE	199 1/8	
Percentage of Irregularity	25.8%	

SIGNAL JAMMER
Ronnie Stevens Buck

Photo courtesy Ronnie Stevens

If you tried to call someone in Columbus, Ohio, between 7:00 and 8 p.m. on Oct. 18, 2011, and got an "all circuits are busy" message, blame Ronnie Stevens.

By the time he'd finished calling all his friends that evening, his telephone was smoking; there was no skin left on his dialing thumb; and he was perilously close to having laryngitis. It's a wonder he didn't lose track of who knew and who didn't know that he'd let the air out of a world-class whitetail.

"I called pretty much everyone in Ohio," he grins.

The bowhunter made short work of putting an arrow through his heart's desire – during his first stint in the new stand – but the 25 days leading up to that long anticipated encounter were anything but routine.

For starters, Ronnie missed opening day of archery season for the first time in 17 years. He had to chauffeur his son to a volleyball game in Sugar Grove.

On the way back home via roads less traveled, he spotted a bachelor group of very nice bucks feeding in a bean field.

"It was only half a mile from where I live," he said. "I immediately stopped, turned around and drove past a second time for another look. One of the bucks was the most incredible 10-pointer I had ever seen afoot. It had to be pushing 180 inches."

So smitten with the deer, Ronnie later went to the Franklin County auditor's office to see who owned the property. He wound up gaining permission to hunt the land and even set up a trail camera over some corn, which snapped several photos of the buck he wanted.

Shortly after setting out the camera, he discovered that the village in which the property is located has a "no projectile" ordinance that applies to arrows as well as shotgun slugs.

A week later, accompanied by friends Steve and Scott Esker, Ronnie attended a council meeting to ask for permission to hunt that farm. When the mayor asked if anyone had any objections, one village man remarked that only residents should be granted such a favor.

Ronnie's request was denied.

"I then decided to back up and punt," he said. "Just across the road was a large CRP field that was inside the city limits of Columbus, where there are no projectile restrictions. So I went back to the auditor's office."

Another knock on a door gained him access to that land, and he wasted no time in hanging a stand and a camera below it.

He pulled the camera's card on Oct. 14 and was thrilled to see the familiar buck with the wide rack.

"I realized the deer was bedding down in a small woodlot at the back of the CRP," Ronnie said. "My setup, which I'd chosen because of the rare climbable tree, was probably within 100 yards of where the big whitetail spent its days.

"It wasn't until the afternoon of Oct. 18 when I felt the wind was right for my stand. I was pumped and ready. I had been looking at pictures of this buck almost daily.

"It was 3:58 when I climbed into my stand. About 6:00, several does came through, feeding slowly as they passed," Ronnie continued. "One of them spotted me when I tried to reposition my legs. I had recently had knee surgery. It was still tender and stiff."

The doe tried to catch him moving again for at least 15 minutes. She would turn her head to look away, and then snap back to peer up into the tree. And then something else stole her attention.

"There was the sound of a branch or twig breaking," Ronnie said. "The doe was looking across the grass field, so I looked that way, too. The wide-racked buck was moving around the perimeter of the CRP.

"It would take a few steps, scent-check, go a few more yards and scent-check again. It kept doing that as it circled closer and closer," he added. "Soon, it was within 18 or 20 yards, but in some thick brush. There was no way for me to get off a shot.

"I was constantly checking the wind with a hand puffer. Five more yards, and the buck was going to be directly downwind of me. It was 6:20 at that point.

"The buck was locked up in a no-shot zone and staring at the does. This went on for an agonizingly long time. Finally, it just turned and walked. I kept looking along the bill of my cap, trying to keep an eye on the deer.

"It circled and started back the same way it had come until it was almost back to where I'd first seen it. I thought the show would soon be over, but the deer suddenly veered right and started coming straight to me," Ronnie said.

"The buck came within range, again, but I still

had no shot. It was so close, my camera shot 14 pictures of it before I could even draw my bow.

"When I finally drew, I knew that deer was dead as soon as the kisser button touched the corner of my mouth. I shot almost straight down, and the arrow blew clean through the deer.

"I felt good; knew I'd hit at least one, if not both lungs," Ronnie said.

"The buck bounded back across the field toward its bedding area, and the does scattered. I was pumped, shaking, and my heart was pounding."

"One of the guys I called reminded me that hunters across the road might cry foul, even though I'd done everything by the book, so I took out my mini camcorder and started videotaping everything around me while I waited for friends to arrive.

"I even videoed myself explaining what had just taken place so it would be on the record, just in case. Then I walked back to the truck, stowed my equipment and waited for the guys.

"They started arriving about 8:10," he added. "When we had enough help, I led them into the CRP to begin the search.

"My trail camera took a picture of all of us fanned out in the woods. A couple of buddies circled the field and were way out close to the woods when I heard a loud scream from one, and then a shout from the other," Ronnie said.

"I was so excited that I took off running and plowed smack into a barbed wire fence. It not only took me down, but it also cut my boot all the way around."

Small price to pay, though.

Photo courtesy Ronnie Stevens

Ronnie Stevens Buck

Official Buckmasters Score Sheet		
Taken by:	**Ronnie Stevens**	
Date:	**October 18, 2011**	
Location:	**Franklin Co., Ohio**	
Method:	**Compound Bow**	
Classification:	**Typical**	
Measurements:	**Right**	**Left**
Total Points Side	5	6
Irregular Points Side	0	0
Total Irregular Inches	0	0
Length of Main Beam	26 3/8	27 3/8
Length of 1st Point	6 7/8	8 3/8
Length of 2nd Point	12 5/8	13 6/8
Length of 3rd Point	10 6/8	11 6/8
Length of 4th Point	7	6 2/8
Length of 5th Point		1 4/8
Length of 6th Point		
1st Circumference (C1)	4 7/8	4 7/8
2nd Circumference (C2)	4 4/8	4 6/8
3rd Circumference (C3)	4 6/8	4 6/8
4th Circumference (C4)	4 4/8	4 4/8
Score Per Side	82 2/8	87 7/8
OFFICIAL SCORE	170 1/8	
Inside Spread	22	
COMPOSITE SCORE	192 1/8	
Percentage of Irregularity	0.0%	

ANTLERS MAXIMUS
Kenny Corwin Buck

Call it kismet.

Had Kenny Corwin arrived at his hunting spot a few minutes earlier or later last December, there would be one more 20-gauge shotshell in his box of slugs and quite a few more dollars in his bank account right now.

In fact, the only thing that didn't work out for the Ohio deer hunter in 2011 was that his kids weren't with him when Lady Luck smiled, which means he didn't get to share the moment. It also meant there was no video footage of the buck that tied his tongue in knots when he called his father after shooting it.

It was his father who had shown him the giant whitetail well into the 2011 season. Kenny was getting ready for an afternoon hunt when Steve Corwin called to tell him a super buck was lying out in a field near their farm.

"I stopped what I was doing and drove the 10 miles down to where Dad and a buddy were watching this buck in a picked bean field," Kenny said. "Sixty yards from the buck was a doe lying beside a fencerow."

Although the animals were 400 yards from the gawkers, the men could tell the buck was enormous even without the aid of binoculars. With glasses, they could tell its tall rack was pushing 200 inches and close to 2 feet wide.

"It was the biggest buck I'd ever seen alive," Kenny said. "It looked to be an 11-pointer, and it was within a quarter—mile of a farm I had permission to hunt. I couldn't help but think it might be bedding in a patch of woods on that farm."

Of course, it could've been wishful thinking, too.

The shotgun opener was just around the corner, and Kenny could think of little else besides the deer he nicknamed Maximus, after his favorite character in the movie "Gladiator."

"Twice during gun season, the wind was right for me to sneak into the patch of woods, but I never saw the buck. There was no reason for him to move very far with all the standing corn, water and green briars."

"During one of those trips, I saw a very impressive 12-pointer that I'd have taken, if given the chance," he continued. "I knew there was going to be three more months for me to bowhunt Maximus. Up to that point, I knew nobody else had taken him, because such a deer's demise would've been big news in our community."

On Sunday, the last day of gun season, the local farmers hit the fields with their combines to harvest the corn, which had been too wet to harvest until then. Every hunter was out to see what might get pushed out of the standing stalks.

It looked like a pumpkin festival with all the orange surrounding the fields.

"A lot of hunters were out there," Kenny said. "A bunch of deer were flushed out, too, but no shots were fired. Nobody saw Maximus, or at least they didn't admit it.

"I bowhunted him three more times in early December, but it was tough getting into the woods because there was no longer any corn to cover my entry. It's a very long walk out in the open," he said.

Kenny began riding his four-wheeler most of the way around the field's perimeter, and then he walked the last few hundred yards to his stand.

Ohio's second gun season was Dec. 17 and 18.

"The first day was a Saturday. My son had basketball practice that morning, and I had to be there to assist, but I was home before noon,"

Kenny said. "As I changed into my hunting clothes, I told my wife I was going to run out, kill this big buck and return in a little while. She knew I was obsessed with getting a shot at this buck.

"It was well past noon when I got to the farm and unloaded the four-wheeler. I started across the field and was going in from a different direction due to the wind," he continued. "When I parked, I noticed a gut pile and was very concerned that someone else had taken Maximus. I found out later that it had belonged to the 12-pointer I saw earlier in the season.

"As I started walking into the wind, I had about 300 yards of open corn stubble to cross to reach the edge of the trees. Around the perimeter is a border of tall Quail Unlimited grass.

"As I was walking up, something looked out of place," he added. "I stopped and thought I could see several long tines sticking above the grass, like a buck's rack" he said.

When Kenny raised his shotgun to peer at the fat grass blades through his scope, he realized he was looking at the buck of his dreams. Maximus was coming out of the thicket, following the same path Kenny had planned to take to his stand.

The deer had to have walked beneath his stand. "If I'd been a few minutes earlier, I might have spooked him; a half-hour later, I would never have seen him. It was as if we were destined to meet," he said.

"So there I was, in the middle of an 80 - acre field of cut corn, and he was headed my way at a steady walk," Kenny continued. "I quickly removed my backpack, placed it on the ground and laid down flat behind it to get what cover I could and also to use it as a gun rest. He didn't see me because he was still in the tall grass."

When Maximus stepped out of the weeds, so did a small 8-pointer. The deer were moving slowly, but definitely getting closer.

"I was hunting with a T/C Encore 20 gauge, sighted-in at 200 yards. But as long as he was getting closer, I saw no need to squeeze the trigger," Kenny said. "I was settled on the deer and tracking his every step.

"Surprisingly, I was dead calm. I even checked

in front of the barrel to make sure I was not going to shoot a corn stalk," he added.

When the buck was about 175 yards from Kenny, it stopped and stared in the hunter's direction, possibly at the strange dirt clod staring back at it.

"I put the crosshairs right on the shoulder, a tad high, and touched off the round," he said. "I hit him in the neck-shoulder area within an inch of where I was aiming. His head went straight up, and he dropped on the spot!

"Suddenly, I wasn't calm anymore," Kenny grinned. "I went completely nuts, shaking like crazy. I called my dad, and he said he would be right there. He later said I'd told him at least five times in the first minute that I'd killed the big one.

"From the minute I first saw this buck, he was on my mind constantly, whether I was hunting or not. I even dreamed about him. Whenever I was off work and the wind was right, I was plotting to tag this buck.

"Destiny brought us together in that stubble," he said.

Photo by Kenny Corwin

Kenny Corwin Buck

Official Buckmasters Score Sheet		
Taken by:	**Kenny Corwin**	
Date:	**December 17, 2011**	
Location:	**Pickaway Co., Ohio**	
Method:	**Shotgun**	
Classification:	**Irregular**	
Measurements:	**Right**	**Left**
Total Points Side	9	9
Irregular Points Side	4	4
Total Irregular Inches	9 7/8	16 5/8
Length of Main Beam	24 5/8	25 3/8
Length of 1st Point	5 6/8	5 4/8
Length of 2nd Point	10 5/8	13 1/8
Length of 3rd Point	10 2/8	9 3/8
Length of 4th Point	4 7/8	6 6/8
Length of 5th Point		
Length of 6th Point		
1st Circumference (C1)	6 3/8	6
2nd Circumference (C2)	4 7/8	5
3rd Circumference (C3)	4 6/8	5
4th Circumference (C4)	4 1/8	4 5/8
Score Per Side	86 1/8	97 3/8
OFFICIAL SCORE	183 4/8	
Inside Spread	23 6/8	
COMPOSITE SCORE	207 2/8	
Percentage of Irregularity	14.4%	

Elk County's Secret is Blown
(and hanging on Joe Dellaquila's wall)
Joe Dellaquila Buck

Photo courtesy Joe Dellaquila

The buck is out of the bag.

Once known primarily for its namesake elk herd, Elk County might have been western Pennsylvania's best-kept secret among Allegheny deer hunters. But that was before Ridgway bowhunter Joe Dellaquila broke the heart of one of the finest whitetails felled north of the Mason-Dixon in 2010.

Joe wasn't the only hunter hoping to get a shot at the buck. While he'd only heard rumors, eventually substantiated by someone's trail camera, many other people had actually seen the giant whitetail.

"I never saw the deer, but I saw pictures of it," he said. "I did lots of scouting, trying to connect the dots and pattern the buck. One person reported seeing it here. A day or two later, it was seen over there.

"I was trying to get a few steps ahead of the buck, and that had me out checking clear-cuts and open fields in the evenings and mornings. Although I never saw the animal, I found some really promising ambush sites on land I could hunt."

Despite all the excitement, Joe found himself with few hours to spare when the season opened. Work and family obligations limited his outings to maybe eight or nine times that first month.

During those trips in October, he saw only two bucks: one not legal under the game commission's three-point (on one side) rule, and the other just barely. Although it has its share of opponents, he has no problem with the restriction.

After working a bit late on Tuesday, Nov. 2, Joe

decided to shelve his planned chores and hit the woods. His wife had taken the kids to raid relatives' leftover Halloween candy in St. Marys. He was supposed to do some trim work on their house.

"When I got home, I could just feel the rut happening out there in the woods. I had to suit up and get out in my stand. It was like the deer were calling me," he said.

Soon after settling into his stand around 5:00, Joe rattled for several seconds and waited.

"I usually wait half an hour between sequences, but since I got a late start, I decided to rattle again after only 15 minutes," he said. "A short time later, I heard a deer walking nearby.

"The buck didn't come charging in, unlike some I've seen," he continued. "This one approached slowly, but steadily, with a stiff-legged walk, passing within 20 yards.

"I attempted to stop it with a couple of quick mouth-bleats, but it just kept moving through," Joe said. "I was at full draw the whole time, and I never had a clear shot. As it kept going away from me, I knew I couldn't let it walk out of my range without at least trying.

"It was moving; severely quartering away from me at about 32 yards. But as soon as it cleared a couple of trees, I released the arrow.

"I saw the arrow hit, and I immediately thought it hadn't penetrated far enough. I was almost sick and angry at myself for taking such a low-percentage shot," he said.

Regardless of how far or little the arrow pierced it, the buck never ran. It kept its pace, circling the hunter of little faith, who was begging the deer gods for another shot.

But that would've been overkill, as the deer stumbled and fell over dead.

"I was in shock," Joe said. "I went from being totally depressed to exhilarated in a matter of seconds. I was so stunned and excited, I couldn't stand. I had to sit down to keep from falling.

"After my nerves settled, I sent a text message to my brother and to a friend, telling them I'd arrowed the big one. Afterward, I got down from the tree and went over to check out the buck.

"When we got it back to my garage, some of my buddies came over to see it. Everybody was texting everybody, I think, and pretty soon there was a small crowd. Before long, some of my friends started putting a tape to the antlers, doing their best to accurately measure it.

"I had one set of pictures of the buck from a trail camera. From those, I'd guessed it would score in the 170s. But my friends, who were reasonably knowledgeable about scoring deer, were tossing out a figure of 200 inches.

"I was totally blown away," he continued.

"I took it to Delullo's Backwoods Taxidermy in Brockport, and he also came up with more than 200 inches," Joe said.

"I won't say that I deserved to shoot this big buck or that I am the best hunter around," Joe said. "But I did my homework and put in a lot of hours, which put me in the right place at the right time. My archery skills did the rest."

Joe took the next day off from work and entered the deer in several big buck contests. At each stop, people gasped, took photographs and wanted to hear his story.

"Everybody wanted to know where I shot it," Joe grinned. "I told them 'Just behind the ribs, going forward.' That's probably not what they wanted to hear, but it's what they got."

Photo courtesy Joe Dellaquila

Joe Dellaquila Buck

Official Buckmasters Score Sheet		
Taken by:	**Joe Dellaquila**	
Date:	**November 2, 2010**	
Location:	**Elk Co., Penna.**	
Method:	**Compound Bow**	
Classification:	**Semi-Irregular**	
Measurements:	**Right**	**Left**
Total Points Side	8	6
Irregular Points Side	2	1
Total Irregular Inches	10	7
Length of Main Beam	26 4/8	25 2/8
Length of 1st Point	6 6/8	0
Length of 2nd Point	12	12 6/8
Length of 3rd Point	9 3/8	11
Length of 4th Point	6 3/8	7 6/8
Length of 5th Point	4 5/8	4 3/8
Length of 6th Point		
1st Circumference (C1)	5 1/8	5
2nd Circumference (C2)	4 1/8	4 2/8
3rd Circumference (C3)	4 2/8	4 5/8
4th Circumference (C4)	4 2/8	4 3/8
Score Per Side	93 3/8	86 3/8
OFFICIAL SCORE	179 6/8	
Inside Spread	22 1/8	
COMPOSITE SCORE	201 7/8	
Percentage of Irregularity	9.4%	

Monster Buck Takes Four 20-Guage Slugs
Clarence Reffitt Buck

Photo Courtesy Ed Waite

On the fifth of Ohio's half-dozen shotgun days in 1999, brothers Clarence and Hermal Reffitt and their cousin, Eric Reffitt, woke at 4 a.m. to allow for the 22-mile drive to their Uncle Jim's Vinton County farm. Each had his own idea of where to be at daybreak.

Eric's destination was closest to the truck, so he veered off first. Clarence and Hermal were going farther into the property, so they kept together until it was time to split. Before the brothers parted company, however, they heard several shots from behind the farm. Soon afterward, a group of does whizzed past them.

Clarence decided to stop there so that he could watch a field from the cover of a fencerow. Hermal hurried down the trail.

After 15 minutes of straining his eyes, Clarence's gaze settled on a dark form standing about 500 yards distant, near a ring of hay in the field's center. There was no doubt that it was a large buck, even though it was well beyond the range of his 20-gauge slug gun.

After several uneasy minutes of just standing there, the nervous buck started across the field, heading for a small gully choked with trees that formed one of the field's borders. Clarence knew that it was a "Keeper" buck, but there was nothing he could do except watch. Shooting would have been futile.

When the buck entered the strip of trees,

Clarence's pulse began racing as it turned in his direction — apparently taking the same path that the nannies had used earlier.

Sure enough, the giant whitetail broke from the trees about 100 yards from Clarence — still cold-trailing the does and moving toward where they had crossed a section of fence.

Just as the buck stopped at the fence, Clarence was dropping to a knee. The hunter took the 80-yard shot before the deer jumped. Afterward, when it tried to clear the fence, it fell to the ground. In a nanosecond, however, the buck was back on its feet and hustling toward a corner. That time, it made the leap — even as two more chunks of lead flew wildly at him. Those last two shots burned only air.

"I reloaded my shotgun, and then I waited for about 5 minutes," Clarence continued. "I could not wait any longer. I knew the buck was hit, but I wasn't sure how bad."

He got a better idea when he found blood indicative of a lung shot.

His strides quickening, Clarence followed the red stuff to where he'd last seen the buck, which was at the crest of a hill. When he got there, he saw the brute with the towering rack lying alongside the fence, next to a large white oak tree.

"I wanted to keep the oak tree between me and the deer as I tried to get closer for another shot," he said. "But when I got to within about 80 yards of him, he saw me and jumped up. Fortunately for me, he got his antlers tangled in the fence's barbed wire. His big drop tine was hooked in the fence, and the buck could not yank it free."

Even with the deer struggling 80 yards in front of him, a thoroughly rattled Clarence somehow managed to miss the frantic target three more times, burning up his last three slugs.

While Clarence was digging around in his pockets, the deer freed itself and took off running again, this time toward a nearby highway. As the frustrated hunter watched his dream buck disappear, he could only hope that the animal would soon exhaust itself and collapse before reaching the road.

Hermal heard all the shooting, and curiosity got the better of him. When he reached Clarence and heard his story, he offered him his 12-gauge to finish the job. But Clarence refused, unwilling to switch to a bigger gun as a point of pride. Instead, he asked his brother to go back to the truck and retrieve some more 20-gauge slugs.

Hermal returned with a handful of shotshells 25 minutes later, and Clarence — in full stalk mode — made his way to the place where he'd last seen the buck.

"I was on a hill that overlooked the nearby highway," Clarence said. "There was a small hollow between me and the road. After scanning the area, I saw my buck lying at the foot of a bank leading up to the road. I was 200 yards from the deer, and he was about 75 yards from the road, which was busy with traffic. He seemed to be watching the cars pass.

"I tried to work my way closer, but because it was very dry in the woods, I could only move when a big truck would pass. Otherwise, there was no way that I could get a safe shot," he added. "I had to get closer!"

Halfway into his slow approach, Clarence suddenly noticed three does standing beside the fallen monarch. He never saw them coming, but he did see them leaving — with the buck in tow.

The buck only made it 10 yards — but closer — before lying down again. The does, meanwhile, continued on toward Clarence. And they spotted him!

"They started snorting and stomping, so I just stood as still as I could.

Then I guess they either saw me move or smelled me, 'cause they stomped again and ran off," Clarence said. "But the buck never moved. He just stayed right there, watching the traffic."

Clarence was still a little too far away for a safe shot, and he was having trouble getting closer without spooking the buck, which was the last thing he wanted to do. He did not want the buck to bust across the busy highway and get slammed by a semi.

Eventually, a pickup truck pulled over to the side of the road, just above the resting buck. It looked like the driver was searching for the deer through a scope or binoculars.

"At first, I thought he was going to let out a hunter. Then I thought that he was just going to haul off and blast the buck from the truck window," Clarence said. "I froze where I was before trying to hide from the truck.

But, at the same time, I did not want him to shoot my deer!"

Finally, after several tense minutes, the truck pulled away from the curb. With the truck's leaving, Clarence's caution also disappeared. He moved in, took a shot from about 75 yards, and hit the buck. He moved 15 yards closer and put another round into it, then sent a third slug into the deer at only 25 yards. He was determined that the buck would not rise again!

Afterward, apparently after hearing the shots, the pickup returned. The driver had been on his way home in a semi when he saw the buck beside the road. When he got home, he grabbed his camera and returned, hoping to take some pictures. Turns out, the guy was an old schoolmate of Clarence's. The two of them field-dressed the deer, loaded it into the truck and drove it back to Uncle Jim's farm.

The Cross Creek check station had been forewarned that a 30-point buck was on its way in to be certified. The local wildlife officer jokingly stated, "I guess I'll need to go in the back and get my high-top boots for this one."

He later ate those words.

Photo Courtesy Ed Waite

Clarence Reffitt Buck

Official Buckmasters Score Sheet		
Taken by:	Clarence Reffitt	
Date:	December 3, 1999	
Location:	Vinton Co., Ohio	
Method:	Shotgun	
Classification:	Irregular	
Measurements:	**Right**	Left
Total Points Side	12	13
Irregular Points Side	6	8
Total Irregular Inches	15	46 5/8
Length of Main Beam	25 2/8	22 1/8
Length of 1st Point	5 6/8	6 4/8
Length of 2nd Point	9 3/8	7 7/8
Length of 3rd Point	9 6/8	9 1/8
Length of 4th Point	8 2/8	10
Length of 5th Point	4 2/8	
Length of 6th Point		
1st Circumference (C1)	5	5 5/8
2nd Circumference (C2)	4 5/8	4 5/8
3rd Circumference (C3)	5 4/8	6
4th Circumference (C4)	5 4/8	6
Score Per Side	98 2/8	124 4/8
OFFICIAL SCORE	222 6/8	
Inside Spread	17 1/8	
COMPOSITE SCORE	239 7/8	
Percentage of Irregularity	27.6%	

There for Anybody to Hunt
Randall Cook Buck

Photo courtesy Ed Waite

Deer Creek State Park in south-central Ohio spans 5,600 acres, a third of it underwater. The nearby Deer Creek Wildlife Area contains another 5,700 acres of timber and meadows: ideal deer habitat.

It was rainy, cold and windy on Nov. 14, 2004, not a good day for a deer hunter to be in the woods. But try telling that to Randy Cook, a shift worker at a car parts factory.

"I kept thinking the rain would stop," Randy defended his decision to brave the elements. "I mean, it was the peak of the rut; Veterans Day. I just felt the need to be out there hunting, even though the weather was not cooperating."

It was about 1:50 when Randy pulled into the public tract's parking area. He then hiked 2 miles to a special spot he'd found while scouting. The place was loaded with buck sign, and a nearby thicket was surely the animals' bedding sanctuary.

Upon arriving at his "perfect spot." Randy set out several film canisters filled with scent near some of the scrapes and rubs.

"I'd scouted and hunted that area before, some in 2005 and a lot in '04." he said. "I knew a nice buck was in there. It was just a matter of IF it would show."

After getting situated in his ground blind, Randy readied his crossbow and settled in for what promised to be a miserable afternoon.

"I tried rattling a couple of times and blew my

doe bleat, but nothing happened except that I got wetter and colder," he said. About every 50 minutes. I rattled in hopes of spurring some action. But all I got was more rain."

About 2 1/2 hours into the hunt, Randy was almost ready to throw in the very wet towel. To make matters worse, the wind was changing direction almost every minute.

"I was getting discouraged and was thinking about leaving. It was after 4:00. and the woods were empty as far as deer were concerned. But then, while I was looking to my left, I heard a noise around the other way. I slowly turned to the right and caught a glimpse of a buck moving out of the thicket about 85 yards away.

"It might have been bedded down in there, because as it cleared the thicket, the deer stopped and shook off the rain.

"Its rack looked really massive as the buck whipped its head back and forth," Randy continued. "My heart started pounding like an alien was coming out of my chest. I'd never seen a buck that big!"

The buck started walking toward the hyperventilating hunter, then it caught a whiff of the scent in one of the canisters. When it got to the canister, which was out about 55 yards, the buck stopped. Its head was behind a tree, which gave Randy the chance to raise his crossbow, at least part of the way.

In a blink, however, the buck whirled around, stepped past the tree and looked straight at Randy for "what seemed like hours." Randy was frozen in place, the crossbow halfway to his shoulder. Finally, the deer lowered its head and started back for the thicket, as if nothing had happened.

"When I grunted, the buck froze," said Randy. "I was shaking so badly, I thought I was going to pass out. I looked through my scope, and it was almost completely fogged over. I could hardly see anything.

"Looking down the side of the scope, and then looking through it, I lined up the shot," he continued. "I guess I lined up on the wrong line, because when I hit the trigger, the bolt hit the deer in the spine."

The buck dropped, but Randy had to finish it. Problem was, he was shaking so violently that he could not get the bolt lined up in the slot. When he did, through no small miracle, a shot to the heart ended the struggle.

"I just dropped everything, ran over to the deer and nudged it in the back to be sure it was down for good," he said. "Then I took the antlers in my hands. I knew it was a monster before I shot, but then it seemed even bigger. I counted 22 points the first time, then 24, and finally settled on 25. (Twenty-two were scoreable.)

Shortly thereafter, another hunter, who had been sitting about 120 yards away, came over to see

Randy's deer.

"Had it not been for that other fellow and another guy who soon came along, I might never have gotten it out of the woods," Randy said. "It was too heavy for me to even budge."

Even with three men dragging the 230-pound (field-dressed) buck back to the parking lot took three hours.

Photo courtesy Ed Waite

Randall Cook Buck

253

Official Buckmasters Score Sheet		
Taken by: Date: Location: Method: Classification:	Randall 'Randy' Cook November 11, 2004 Fayette Co., Ohio Crossbow Irregular	
Measurements:	**Right**	**Left**
Total Points Side	10	12
Irregular Points Side	5	7
Total Irregular Inches	6 6/8	16 5/8
Length of Main Beam	27 7/8	27 3/8
Length of 1st Point	4 1/8	6 4/8
Length of 2nd Point	11 1/8	12
Length of 3rd Point	9 7/8	9 6/8
Length of 4th Point	6 5/8	4 5/8
Length of 5th Point		
Length of 6th Point		
1st Circumference (C1)	5	5 2/8
2nd Circumference (C2)	5 3/8	5 1/8
3rd Circumference (C3)	5 3/8	4 6/8
4th Circumference (C4)	4 6/8	4
Score Per Side	86 7/8	96
OFFICIAL SCORE	182 7/8	
Inside Spread	19 3/8	
COMPOSITE SCORE	202 2/8	
Percentage of Irregularity	12.8%	

The Buck with the Jekyll & Hyde Rack
Jeff Yelton Buck

Photo by Jeff Yelton

Powerless to do anything but gawk, Jeff Yelton's gaze shifted back and forth from the deer with the strange rack to his watch. Always one to follow the rules, the hunter from Chesterton, Ind., knew it wasn't yet light enough to legally squeeze his muzzleloader's trigger.

He was almost convinced something was wrong with his too- slow watch.

He KNEW something was wrong with the animal's antlers.

The left side of the rack was normal, if not extraordinary. If Jeff had bothered to count the points, he'd have tallied six long (typical) ones on that side alone.

But it was the right side that kept him from counting, and which demanded attention. All that junk couldn't be antler, could it?

This brief encounter occurred four days before Jeff's question was answered.

Jeff and a couple of friends hunt property in Porter County that's bordered by a nearly 400-foot-long power company right-of-way and an underground pipeline. They've acquired permission to plant several food plots on the right-of-ways.

"I first encountered this buck on the Wednesday before Thanksgiving," he said. "It came out of the adjacent property we call 'the preserve,' private ground owned by a fellow in Chicago who doesn't allow hunting.

"It was early, about 50 minutes before legal

shooting light, when the buck came to within 20 yards of my stand," Jeff continued. "I was sitting there on pins and needles the whole time. It stopped next to a fallen log where I'd spread some estrous doe lure, and didn't seem to know I was there."

Jeff kept an eye on his watch, willing the minute hand to move faster.

"It wound up walking straight north and away from me," he said.

Because of the poor light, Jeff couldn't tell exactly what was different about the buck's rack. The left side seemed normal, but the right seemed off-kilter. There was a mass close to its head.

"I thought it might be carrying some brush or tangled briars," he said.

Only when the deer was leaving was Jeff able to get a closer look through binoculars, and that's when he realized the mass was antler, not vegetation. And he was crushed.

On the Monday after Thanksgiving, after he'd worked the weekend, Jeff was back in his stand before sunrise. Before shooting light, he saw a familiar doe come into the field. She was recognizable because of her three fawns.

"About 7:40, I saw a pretty big buck come out about 400 yards away. I lowered my binoculars and cradled my muzzleloader in my lap," he said.

"The buck was walking parallel to the strip of trees in which I was sitting, but I lost sight of it because of all the undergrowth.

"My attention was on that deer when, all of a sudden, I heard a snort behind me. When I turned to look, I saw the flash of antlers near another stand about 150 yards distant.

'I'm thinking: the wind is wrong for him to be smelling me. Something else must be causing his alarm.

"I thought the second buck was approaching from the bean field side of the fencerow. I heard a couple more snorts and a snort-wheeze — closer that time — and then silence," he continued.

Eventually, Jeff saw the buck coming through a gap in the fence line, followed by a doe. It was the one with the junk around the base of its right antler, coming his way.

"I'd gun- and bowhunted from that ladder stand for many years, and I'd ranged just about every twig and tree," Jeff said. "There are several Russian olive trees, one at 80 yards and another at 120.

"When the buck approached the nearest one, I got down on one knee to steady myself and to use the stand's side rail as a rest. As soon as it cleared the tree, I grunted.

"I centered the crosshairs on the buck's shoulder when it stopped," he added.

Jeff thought he saw the buck kick after the shot, but he wasn't sure because of the smoke. A second or two later, he saw it and the doe running for the woods.

"I waited 30 minutes or so, and then headed for the olive tree," Jeff said. "I didn't see any blood or hair, and I wondered if I'd somehow missed."

Just to be sure he hadn't misjudged things, Jeff walked the 40 yards to the next olive tree, eyes riveted to the ground. But there was no sign whatsoever.

On his way back to the first tree, he happened to glance toward a tangle of multiflora rose and saw a fingernail—sized drop of blood. He also saw some hair.

"From there, I walked a straight line to the woods and saw nothing along the route. So I returned to that one drop of blood," he said. "When I scoured the area, I discovered a huge puddle of blood in the grass. I can't imagine how I missed it earlier."

From there, Jeff followed the trail to his deer, which had careened into a tree soon after entering the woods.

Photo by Jeff Yelton

Jeff Yelton Buck

Official Buckmasters Score Sheet		
Taken by:	**Jeff Yelton**	
Date:	**November 26, 2012**	
Location:	**Porter Co., Indiana**	
Method:	**Blackpowder**	
Classification:	**Irregular**	
Measurements:	**Right**	**Left**
Total Points Side	10	6
Irregular Points Side	5	0
Total Irregular Inches	36 5/8	0
Length of Main Beam	21 2/8	21 6/8
Length of 1st Point	9 5/8	5 1/8
Length of 2nd Point	10 4/8	13 1/8
Length of 3rd Point	7 1/8	9 7/8
Length of 4th Point	4	6 4/8
Length of 5th Point		3 6/8
Length of 6th Point		
1st Circumference (C1)	4 3/8	4 5/8
2nd Circumference (C2)	4 5/8	4 6/8
3rd Circumference (C3)	3 4/8	4 6/8
4th Circumference (C4)	3 3/8	4 6/8
Score Per Side	105	79
OFFICIAL SCORE	184	
Inside Spread	14 7/8	
COMPOSITE SCORE	198 7/8	
Percentage of Irregularity	19.9%	

CARPE DEERUM
Andrew Cooper Buck

Photo courtesy Ed Waite

Given the choice between going to a classroom and taking a final exam or spending opening morning of the firearms season in a treestand, is there any doubt which a deer hunter will do?

For Andrew Cooper of Hillsborough, Ohio, the decision wasn't exactly a no-brainer. Until the moment he went to bed on Nov. 28, he was torn between his desire to be afield and his yearning to put the test, for which he'd studied long and hard, behind him.

But the weather forecast for Highland County was perfect for Monday morning, and his accounting instructor had said the final exam could be taken on Wednesday.

He went hunting.

"My parents have a small farm, just 77 acres, and my grandparents own a 160-acre farm nearby, so I had lots of land to hunt," Andrew said. "I am not a serious bone hunter; just a meat-for-the-freezer guy, for the most part. I've never used trail cameras until this past year; never tried food plots. By today's standards, I'm not a good example of a dedicated deer hunter."

That doesn't mean, of course, that size is unimportant.

"We try to manage our farm for quality deer to the extent we can," he said. "But most of the neighboring landowners don't care as much as we do about harvesting only mature deer.

"We try to manage the does and don't shoot button bucks," he continued. "We ask those who hunt on our land to hold out for bucks in the 130-inch or larger range. There are a lot of transient deer that are here today and somewhere else tomorrow."

Several hunters have been granted access to the land Andrew hunts, and there are quite a few stands – available to everyone – that have been erected.

"A few of the folks only bowhunt, so they are not here for the gun season," he said. "Since I was going after my college degree, I didn't really have time to bowhunt."

When Andrew set out that Monday, Nov. 29, he chose to sit in a lock-on-type stand about 15 yards inside the woods flanking a CRP field.

"The field is to the right of the stand. A large cedar grove is about 50 yards to the left of it. The thin strip of hardwoods in which the stand is located is a nice pinch point," he said.

"For whatever reason, there had been only a handful of nice bucks spotted over the five years that the stand was in place, and none had been harvested. Only does had been taken there in recent years," he continued. "Nevertheless, it always struck me as a prime spot. I just had a feeling that was the place to be, and I was aloft before sunrise."

It was an incredibly quiet morning. By 8:00, Andrew had heard on a scattering of shots emanating from the surrounding farms.

"I couldn't help but wonder if the day was going to be a total bust," he said. "While wondering if I should've gone to class instead, I heard a loud crash in the woods behind me. I turned slightly to look, but saw nothing.

"When I stood and twisted around to get a better look, I saw a huge rack rising above the weeds," he added. "My adrenal gland just about exploded. I never expected to see a deer of that size standing just 40 yards away!"

Andrew couldn't see the entire buck. Only its shoulder, neck and head were visible. Although he wanted very badly to shoot the deer, there simply was no shot.

"I quietly twisted back around, facing away from the buck, and then I started turning my feet so my whole body would be facing it," he said. "I was more than halfway turned when the stand creaked loudly and I just knew I was busted. I turned my head until I was facing the giant, but it hadn't moved."

The buck might've heard the noise, but it apparently fought the urge to flee until it discovered the source.

"Fortunately, I had the tree to help conceal my movement. While the buck was frozen in place and on high alert, I finished my turn, brought my open-sighted 20 gauge to my shoulder and braced against the trunk," Andrew said. "I needed the deer to take one or two steps into the open.

"The longer I waited, the more nervous I became," he continued. "I was afraid the buck would bolt without offering me the shot I wanted, so afraid that I decided to aim for where its thick neck met shoulder."

The big whitetail surged forward at the shot, but it collapsed almost immediately. To seal the deal, Andrew shot it a second time.

"I waited 30 or so minutes, watching the downed buck while I called people," he said. "After about the third or fourth call, I looked up and couldn't see my buck anymore. I nearly panicked until I realized I was looking in the wrong place.

"After that little shock, I lowered my gun and clumsily got down from the stand. I had no idea there was such an animal on our farm," Andrew added.

Because the buck fell close to the field's edge, Andrew was able to drive his truck close to it. Some friends helped him load it.

Photo courtesy Andrew Cooper

Andrew Cooper Buck

Official Buckmasters Score Sheet		
Taken by:	**Andrew Cooper**	
Date:	**November 29, 2010**	
Location:	**Highland Co., Ohio**	
Method:	**Shotgun**	
Classification:	**Irregular**	
Measurements:	**Right**	**Left**
Total Points Side	9	7
Irregular Points Side	4	2
Total Irregular Inches	15	12 4/8
Length of Main Beam	29 1/8	27 1/8
Length of 1st Point	6 5/8	9 4/8
Length of 2nd Point	7 6/8	14 2/8
Length of 3rd Point	9 6/8	11 3/8
Length of 4th Point	3 6/8	2 4/8
Length of 5th Point		
Length of 6th Point		
1st Circumference (C1)	4 7/8	5 5/8
2nd Circumference (C2)	4 4/8	4 5/8
3rd Circumference (C3)	4 7/8	5 1/8
4th Circumference (C4)	3 7/8	4
Score Per Side	90 1/8	96 5/8
OFFICIAL SCORE	186 6/8	
Inside Spread	20 3/8	
COMPOSITE SCORE	207 1/8	
Percentage of Irregularity	14.7%	

Thank you for taking the time to read this little compilation of stories.

Be on the lookout for Volume II

Coming soon!